F. SCOTT FITZGERALD

COMPREHENSIVE RESEARCH
AND STUDY GUIDE

BLOOM'S

MAJOR
NOVELISTS

EDITED AND WITH AN
INTRODUCTION BY HAROLD BLOOM

BLOOM'S MAJOR DRAMATISTS

Anton Chekhov
Henrik Ibsen
Arthur Miller
Eugene O'Neill
Shakespeare's Comedies
Shakespeare's Histories
Shakespeare's Romances
Shakespeare's Tragedies
George Bernard Shaw
Tennessee Williams

BLOOM'S MAJOR NOVELISTS

Jane Austen
The Brontës
Willa Cather
Charles Dickens
William Faulkner
F. Scott Fitzgerald
Nathaniel Hawthorne
Ernest Hemingway
Toni Morrison
John Steinbeck
Mark Twain
Alice Walker

BLOOM'S MAJOR SHORT STORY WRITERS

William Faulkner
F. Scott Fitzgerald
Ernest Hemingway
O. Henry
James Joyce
Herman Melville
Flannery O'Connor
Edgar Allan Poe
J. D. Salinger
John Steinbeck
Mark Twain
Eudora Welty

BLOOM'S MAJOR WORLD POETS

Geoffrey Chaucer
Emily Dickinson
John Donne
T. S. Eliot
Robert Frost
Langston Hughes
John Milton
Edgar Allan Poe
Shakespeare's Poems & Sonnets
Alfred, Lord Tennyson
Walt Whitman
William Wordsworth

BLOOM'S NOTES

The Adventures of Huckleberry Finn
Aeneid
The Age of Innocence
Animal Farm
The Autobiography of Malcolm X
The Awakening
Beloved
Beowulf
Billy Budd, Benito Cereno, & Bartleby the Scrivener
Brave New World
The Catcher in the Rye
Crime and Punishment
The Crucible

Death of a Salesman
A Farewell to Arms
Frankenstein
The Grapes of Wrath
Great Expectations
The Great Gatsby
Gulliver's Travels
Hamlet
Heart of Darkness & The Secret Sharer
Henry IV, Part One
I Know Why the Caged Bird Sings
Iliad
Inferno
Invisible Man
Jane Eyre
Julius Caesar

King Lear
Lord of the Flies
Macbeth
A Midsummer Night's Dream
Moby-Dick
Native Son
Nineteen Eighty-Four
Odyssey
Oedipus Plays
Of Mice and Men
The Old Man and the Sea
Othello
Paradise Lost
The Portrait of a Lady
A Portrait of the Artist as a Young Man

Pride and Prejudice
The Red Badge of Courage
Romeo and Juliet
The Scarlet Letter
Silas Marner
The Sound and the Fury
The Sun Also Rises
A Tale of Two Cities
Tess of the D'Urbervilles
Their Eyes Were Watching God
To Kill a Mockingbird
Uncle Tom's Cabin
Wuthering Heights

F. SCOTT FITZGERALD

COMPREHENSIVE RESEARCH
AND STUDY GUIDE

BLOOM'S

MAJOR
NOVELISTS

EDITED AND WITH AN INTRODUCTION
BY HAROLD BLOOM

Printed and bound in the United States of America.

3 5 7 9 8 6 4 2

Library of Congress Cataloging-in-Publication Data
F. Scott Fitzgerald / edited and with an introduction by Harold Bloom.
    p.   cm. — (Bloom's major novelists)
  Includes bibliographical references and index.
  ISBN 0-7910-5254-0
  1. Fitzgerald, F. Scott (Francis Scott), 1896–1940—Examinations—
Study guides.   I. Bloom, Harold.   II. Title: Francis Scott
Fitzgerald.   III. Series.
PS3511.I9Z61374   1999
813'.52—dc21   99–27013
                                                           CIP

Chelsea House Publishers
1974 Sproul Road, Suite 400
Broomall, PA 19008-0914

The Chelsea House World Wide Web address is
www.chelseahouse.com

Contributing Editor: Pearl James

Contents

User's Guide

This volume is designed to present biographical, critical, and bibliographical information on the author's best-known or most important works. Following Harold Bloom's editor's note and introduction are a detailed biography of the author, discussing major life events and important literary accomplishments. A plot summary of each novel follows, tracing significant themes, patterns, and motifs in the work.

A selection of critical extracts, derived from previously published material from leading critics, analyzes aspects of each work. The extracts consist of statements from the author, if available, early reviews of the work, and later evaluations up to the present. A bibliography of the author's writings (including a complete list of all works written, cowritten, edited, and translated), a list of additional books and articles on the author and his or her work, and an index of themes and ideas in the author's writings conclude the volume.

~

Harold Bloom is Sterling Professor of the Humanities at Yale University and Henry W. and Albert A. Berg Professor of English at the New York University Graduate School. He is the author of over 20 books and the editor of more than 30 anthologies of literary criticism.

Professor Bloom's works include *Shelley's Mythmaking* (1959), *The Visionary Company* (1961), *Blake's Apocalypse* (1963), *Yeats* (1970), *A Map of Misreading* (1975), *Kabbalah and Criticism* (1975), and *Agon: Toward a Theory of Revisionism* (1982). *The Anxiety of Influence* (1973) sets forth Professor Bloom's provocative theory of the literary relationships between the great writers and their predecessors. His most recent books include *The American Religion* (1992), *The Western Canon* (1994), *Omens of Millennium: The Gnosis of Angels, Dreams, and Resurrection* (1996), and *Shakespeare: The Invention of the Human* (1998), a finalist for the 1998 National Book Award.

Professor Bloom earned his Ph.D. from Yale University in 1955 and has served on the Yale faculty since then. He is a 1985 MacArthur Foundation Award recipient, served as the Charles Eliot Norton Professor of Poetry at Harvard University in 1987–88, and has received honorary degrees from the universities of Rome and Bologna. In 1999, Professor Bloom received the prestigious American Academy of Arts and Letters Gold Medal for Criticism.

Currently, Harold Bloom is the editor of numerous Chelsea House volumes of literary criticism, including the series BLOOM'S NOTES, BLOOM'S MAJOR SHORT STORY WRITERS, BLOOM'S MAJOR POETS, MAJOR LITERARY CHARACTERS, MODERN CRITICAL VIEWS, MODERN CRITICAL INTERPRETATIONS, AND WOMEN WRITERS OF ENGLISH AND THEIR WORKS.

Editor's Note

I particularly recommend Malcolm Cowley, Marius Bewley, Leo Marx, and David L. Minter on *The Great Gatsby*. Illuminating views of *Tender Is the Night* include those of William Doherty, James Gindin, Brian Way, and Judith Fetterly.

Introduction

HAROLD BLOOM

After three-quarters of a century, *The Great Gatsby* remains a fresh and vibrant short novel, an acknowledged American masterpiece. Its fable has become part of the American mythology, or perhaps the American Dream so pervades *The Great Gatsby* that Fitzgerald's true achievement was to appropriate American legend. Either way, Fitzgerald gave us both the romance of love-and-money, and the anti-romance of its collapse into tragedy, if "tragedy" does not seem too exalted a term for Jay Gatsby. The book is profoundly Conradian, since Nick Carraway mediates Gatsby for us rather in the way that Joseph Conrad's Marlow mediates Kurtz or Lord Jim. We do not see, hear, or know Gatsby except through Carraway's eyes, ears, and heart, and for Nick his friend Jay is the Romantic hero of the American Dream.

For Carraway, Gatsby is an idealist, with a "Platonic conception of himself." Time, other selves, history: all these are set aside by Gatsby's vision of himself and the perfectly insipid Daisy Buchanan as the American Adam and Eve. Gatsby himself is an improbable but persuasive amalgam of an American gangster and the poet John Keats, dreaming an impossible dream of love with *his* Daisy, Fanny Brawne. Gatsby is great, not just in Carraway's vision, but in ours, because Fitzgerald brilliantly represents in Gatsby both the failure of the American Dream and its perpetual refusal to die.

Tender Is the Night, with its Keatsian title, was intended by Fitzgerald to be his masterwork. Though the novel is at least partly a failure, it is a fascinating debacle, intensely readable though somewhat diffuse. Dick Diver is a pale figure when compared to Gatsby; the reader cannot help liking Diver, but he lacks Gatsby's obsessive force. Is Diver defeated by the rich, who fascinate him, or by his own inner weakness? Rather clearly, Diver is Fitzgerald's own surrogate, as Gatsby never was. Diver fails and dwindles away because of a weakness in the will, in profound contrast to Gatsby. Perhaps all that could have saved *Tender Is the Night* would have been Jay Gatsby's resurrection from the dead, since the gangster-poet's vitality never possesses Dick Diver. ❁

Biography of
F. Scott Fitzgerald

Francis Scott Key Fitzgerald was born in St. Paul, Minnesota, in 1896 to Edward and Mary McQuillan Fitzgerald. His mother, Mary McQuillan, was descended from Irish immigrants who had come to the United States during the years of famine in Ireland (1840–50). The McQuillan family had made a profitable grocery enterprise in St. Paul. His father, Edward Fitzgerald, came from Maryland and, on his mother's side, could trace his family back to the colonial period and to such famous ancestors as Scott's namesake, Francis Scott Key (author of "The Star Spangled Banner"). Although Mary inherited a good living, the Fitzgerald family had difficulty maintaining the high standard of middle-class life to which they had been bred. A sister, Annabel, was born in 1901. The family lived in Buffalo and in Syracuse, New York, but eventually settled permanently near the maternal side of the family in St. Paul.

Scott Fitzgerald showed literary talent at an early age. He kept a written record of his early impressions and experiences, and developed his ability as a keen social observer. As a teenager in St. Paul, he wrote mysteries for his school paper and plays for amateur productions. Eventually his parents sent him to the Newman School in New Jersey, a small Catholic preparatory school. There, he struggled for (and never quite achieved) popularity, and also pursued his writing. He formed a strong attachment to a priest, Father Sigourney Fay, a well-educated and cultured man. Father (eventually Monsignor) Fay encouraged Fitzgerald's interest in literature, and was something of a role model for Fitzgerald, who briefly considered becoming a priest.

From the Newman School, Fitzgerald went to Princeton University. He loved Princeton's privileged atmosphere and its Gothic architecture but he was never a particularly good student. He dreamed of being a football star but at 5' 7", he lacked the necessary physique. However he continued to write stories, poems, plays, and song lyrics and he was involved with several dramatic productions produced by the Princeton Triangle Club, although his grades made it difficult for him to participate as much as he would have liked. He formed lasting friendships with John Peale Bishop and Edmund

("Bunny") Wilson; both shared his interest in literature and exerted strong influence on his development as a reader. He fell in love with a debutante, Ginevra King, and had a lively social life of dances, parties, and visits. A combination of poor study habits and illness required Fitzgerald to take a leave of absence and to forfeit the presidency of the Cottage Club and performance in a Triangle show he had coauthored—all long-felt disappointments.

When the United States entered World War I in 1917, Fitzgerald enlisted and received a commission as an infantry second lieutenant. During his training, he spent his weekends working on his first novel, *The Romantic Egoist*. While stationed near Montgomery, Alabama, he attended a dance and met the woman that would become his wife, Zelda Sayre. Zelda was a wild-spirited, fun, spoiled, and beautiful girl—the last child born to a judge and his wife. Zelda shared Fitzgerald's ambitions, and wanted a larger purview than the small-town life available in Montgomery. They quickly fell in love. The war ended before Fitzgerald's unit was sent abroad (another disappointment), and after being discharged in 1919, he went to New York to make his fortune and earn Zelda's hand. After a few months of grinding work in advertising, drinking bouts, and having his literary submissions rejected, it seemed that he and Zelda would not be able to marry. She broke off their engagement, and Fitzgerald went home to St. Paul, where he revised his novel. That fall, success began to come his way: his novel (now called *This Side of Paradise*) was accepted, he published several stories, and he found a literary agent, Harold Ober. In 1920, he and Zelda were married in New York. *This Side of Paradise* became an overnight success, and the Fitzgeralds found themselves in the midst of an exuberant and fashionable social scene, in which they played a starring role as a dashing and wild young couple. They lived in France in the early 1920s in a circle of American expatriates that included Ernest Hemingway and Gertrude Stein.

Scott and Zelda Fitzgerald shared a penchant for excess—financial, alcoholic, emotional—that made their married life tumultuous, exciting, and difficult. They traveled a great deal and lived in hotels and rented flats and houses in Europe, New York, and, occasionally, near their relatives. They had a daughter, Scottie, in 1921. Fitzgerald wrote and sold short stories for considerable amounts of money, and struggled to find time for his novels, which required long periods of concentrated work. He published *The Beautiful and Damned* to some critical and financial success in 1922. His greatest novel, *The Great Gatsby*, published in 1925, was not a best-seller but was recognized, by some, as a masterpiece. In between novels, his publisher, Charles Scribner, collected the short stories, some of which were also marketed to the film studios in Hollywood. His next novel, *Tender Is the Night*, took several years to finish, and was not published until 1934.

A frustrated artist herself, Zelda Fitzgerald wrote, danced, and painted. She suffered the first of several mental and emotional breakdowns in 1930. Fitzgerald drank heavily, which exacerbated his ability to cope with her illness. Their economic imprudence also made things difficult. By 1934, Zelda was hospitalized for longer and longer periods of time, and the day-to-day responsibilities of Scottie's upbringing were left in the hands of family, friends, and her boarding school. By 1937, Fitzgerald's great financial debts to his agent and his publisher prompted him to go to Hollywood and work for MGM as a screen writer. He found the work tedious and aggravating, and relieved his frustration in a series of satirical stories about a hack writer called Pat Hobby. There he met Sheilah Graham, a Hollywood gossip columnist, who became his companion. His drinking, although still a problem, was more controlled than it had been for much of the 1920s and 1930s. He died of a heart attack in 1940, while working on his fifth novel, *The Last Tycoon*. It was published posthumously, as were collections of his stories and essays. In the 1960s his work received new attention, and his literary reputation as a major American writer became assured. ✾

Plot Summary of
The Great Gatsby

When *The Great Gatsby* was published in 1925, the novel did not sell well. Disappointing sales, however, were counteracted by some serious and positive critical commentary. After Fitzgerald's death in 1940, his work—particularly *The Great Gatsby*—received increasing attention, and *Gatsby* is now considered a classic.

Gatsby has a quintessentially "modern" setting and group of characters: Fitzgerald sets this novel in his own time and milieu of middle- and upper-middle-class white Americans. Fitzgerald pictured himself as the voice of his generation and wrote for a young audience—those people "about the same age" as the twentieth century itself. *Gatsby* is both a coming-of-age story and a record of social phenomena in the 1920s: drinking during Prohibition; the new place of automobiles in society; an entertainment world peopled by photographers, film directors and stars, and jazz bands; female professionals like Jordan Baker; and changing attitudes toward social institutions (i.e., marriage). In his observation of the manners around him, the novel's narrator, Nick Carraway, famously remarks that he is "within and without, simultaneously enchanted and repelled by the inexhaustible variety of life." This position has been ascribed to Fitzgerald as a writer ever since.

Gatsby has the most tightly constructed plot of any of Fitzgerald's novels. The novel's events unfold in a summer and are remembered in retrospect by the narrator, Nick. This frame enables a complicated narrative tone: Nick tells the reader what happens, and also reckons with his feelings about what happened. This dimension—how Nick's memory and emotions influence the story—must be kept in mind by the reader. For although he presents himself as "honest," his presentation of the story contains omissions. Nick warns us directly: "I have been drunk just twice in my life and the second time was that afternoon, so everything that happened has a dim hazy cast over it . . . " The "dim cast" of alcohol is compounded by the process of selection writing requires: "Reading over what I have written so far I see that I have given the impression that the events of three nights several weeks apart were all that absorbed me. On the contrary they were merely casual events in a crowded summer . . . " Furthermore, critics question

Nick's reliability as a narrator on the grounds that he is more involved in the events than he pretends, and his feelings have clouded his representations of various characters. Other critics notice that although Fitzgerald's use of the first-person narrator had improved in this work, he occasionally slips into an omniscient voice, violating the reader's sense that this story belongs to Nick.

Why does Nick tell this story? According to him, he plays a minor role, and "the history of the summer really begins on the evening I drove over [to East Egg] to have dinner with the Tom Buchanans." Eventually, Nick forms a connection between the Buchanans' conservative social world in East Egg and that of his nouveau riche neighbor in West Egg, Jay Gatsby. Yet Nick pictures himself primarily as an observer, one who vows to set "the record" straight. He tells Gatsby's story since Gatsby, being dead, cannot speak for himself.

Who is Gatsby? Why is he so compelling? Nick worries that Gatsby has been misunderstood, that his death has not been properly memorialized. Gatsby remains a mysterious figure. Although Nick writes to explain Gatsby, his narrative ironically suggests that Gatsby can never fully be known. Rumors circulate about him: "Somebody told me they thought he killed a man once," says one party-goer; "It's more that he was a German spy during the war," rejoins another. Although Nick vows to give the reader the real story, Gatsby's identity remains elusive.

The elusiveness of Gatsby's character suggests that he serves an allegorical purpose: he is more symbol than person. In fact, Gatsby may symbolize a general principle of chaos—the fact that social and narrative rules are perpetually broken in the novel's new, modern, postwar world. At Gatsby's party, his appearance startles Nick, who explains, "I had expected that Mr. Gatsby would be a florid and corpulent person in his middle years." Instead, Nick sees "an elegant young rough-neck, a year or two over thirty, whose elaborate formality of speech just missed being absurd." Gatsby disappoints Nick's expectation by not being an older, obviously self-indulgent, stereotypical millionaire. On the other hand, Gatsby replaces Nick's false presupposition with a "reality" that does not fit either. Gatsby's identity refuses to cohere, he remains internally contradictory: "an elegant . . . rough-neck."

As this particular oxymoron suggests, Gatsby's confusing identity has a relation to social class. From this perspective, the obscurity of his origins has a literal referent: poor origins. Gatsby symbolizes the specific disruption of class boundaries. Like Horatio Alger protagonists, Gatsby lives a rags-to-riches dream. Born as James Gatz in the Midwest to "shiftless and unsuccessful farm people," he leaves his family as a young man to make his own way. He meets Dan Cody, a character out of the Old West, a self-made man, who becomes a surrogate father. But Gatsby's identity, like his name, "[springs] from his Platonic conception of himself" even before he encounters Cody. Fitzgerald's invocation of Plato—an original Utopian visionary—reminds the reader how idealistic the American myth of the self-made man is. Gatsby encapsulates the naivete and hopefulness of the best American promises: to rise above one's birth, to achieve greatness and personal dreams through perseverance. Ultimately, Gatsby fails to realize his dreams, and part of Fitzgerald's purpose in the novel seems to be to signify the limits of the American myth.

Although Gatsby ultimately fails to achieve his dreams, the novel does not show other, more successful or more virtuous, self-made men. Tom Buchanan, who has what Gatsby wants as if by right, is hardly an ideal. He has not come by his wealth through work. He makes just as conspicuous a show of his money as Gatsby: "his freedom with money was a matter for reproach— . . . he'd left Chicago and come east in a fashion that rather took your breath away . . . " As the heir to American wealth and the member of an aristocratic social class, Buchanan serves as Gatsby's counterpoint, but Gatsby benefits by the comparison. Tom abuses his power: he cheats on his wife, he physically abuses his mistress, he schemes and uses Wilson as a pawn to eliminate Gatsby in the end. The spectacle of his power and his "cruel body" command our attention, but he can hardly be accorded admiration or respect. Fitzgerald uses East Egg as a counterpoint to West Egg, and he uses Buchanan's inherited wealth as if to emphasize the gaudiness of Gatsby's acquired wealth. Gatsby's source of income is almost certainly criminal, as his connection to Meyer Wolfshiem (the man who "fixed the World Series") suggests. But the novel suggests that inherited wealth is not only not better than money acquired through speculation or criminal means—it may actually be worse. Their money makes the Buchanans careless and dangerous: "they were careless people, Tom and Daisy—they smashed up things and creatures and then retreated back into their money," Nick tells the reader.

Gatsby pursues a symbolic version of the American dream: he dreams of Daisy rather than of wealth for its own sake. He uses his money to woo Daisy as if the intervening years had never happened. He refuses to recognize the force of history and the fact that one "can't repeat the past." When Daisy and Gatsby first met, he could not really expect her to marry him since he was poor. Daisy has come to mean more to Gatsby than she did once upon a time. "Her voice is full of money": that is the real essence of "the inexhaustible charm that rose and fell in it, the jingle of it, the cymbals' song of it. . . . High in a white palace the king's daughter, the golden girl. . . . " Daisy has become the holy grail, the object of a knightly quest, the reward in a fairy-tale romance. Gatsby's wishing star is a little green light: literally, it identifies the Buchanans' dock, but it also shares the color of money. Daisy unites several symbolic desires.

Critics complain that Gatsby remains too vague a character, and the same can be said of Daisy. This vagueness may or may not have been intentional, but it reveals something important about them. Both Daisy and Gatsby belong in a simpler world, or in some other kind of story: some "Hopalong Cassidy" or romance, where boys are adventurous heroes and girls are fairy princesses. So Daisy wishes for her daughter: "I hope she'll be a fool—that's the best thing a girl can be in this world, a beautiful little fool." She wishes that her daughter will not have to reckon with the "cruel" and disappointing realities of modern life as she has. Their mutual naivete contributes to the novel's tragic dimension. Marriage to Tom has been a series of humiliations for Daisy, and Gatsby seems to offer her the dream that she might be young and hopeful again. However, divorce does not seem to be a viable option, and Daisy's affair ultimately brings her closer to Tom. The consolidation of the Buchanan marriage marks the beginning of the end. From a certain perspective, the fact that Daisy drives the car that accidentally kills her rival for Tom seems oddly like an assertion of self, a claim to her rights as a wife. Fitzgerald's exploration of marriage's destructive effects on men and women ultimately gets subsumed into his larger critique of money's destructive power. ❀

List of Characters in
The Great Gatsby

Nick Carraway is the novel's first-person narrator. He turns thirty during the summer. Having fought in World War I, he feels "restless" and decides to leave his home in the Midwest to go East and learn the bond business. There, he works in New York City but lives in West Egg on Long Island. Compared to Jay Gatsby and Tom Buchanan, Nick has modest means and modest desires. His status as a narrator, living both inside and outside the story's events, has been avidly debated by critics of the novel.

Jay Gatsby (born James Gatz), the hero who gives the novel its name, is a dreamer. He loves Daisy Buchanan, and has amassed a fortune in hopes of winning her away from her husband. His vast wealth spawns increasingly fantastic rumors: that he ran a chain of drugstores, that he is a bootlegger, that he commits criminal activities including murder. He is generous as a neighbor and as a host, issuing invitations and creating pleasure for others. His large and lavish parties last through the night and are attended by New York's fashionable social circles. Despite his popularity, however, Gatsby lives a secretive life, keeping his past and his secret love for Daisy to himself.

Daisy Buchanan is Nick Carraway's distant cousin and the golden girl of Gatsby's dreams. She is married to Tom Buchanan and lives an unhappy, bored life as his wife. She has a daughter, but her role as a mother is minimal since she is wealthy and has servants to raise her child. Although she loves Gatsby, she does not pretend that she had never loved Tom. She refuses to divorce Tom. She drives the "death car" that kills Myrtle Wilson, and she—at least indirectly—contributes to the cause of Gatsby's death.

Tom Buchanan, whom Gatsby introduces at his party as "the polo player," is a brutal figure. He has a large capacity for violence and duplicity. His lack of intelligence contributes to his sense of powerlessness, which in turn feeds his violence. Tom's xenophobia and his paranoia manifest themselves in a confused appreciation of pseudo-scientific, apocalyptic fantasies: "Civilization's going to pieces," broke out Tom violently. "I've gotten to be a terrible pessimist about things. Have you read 'The Rise of the Colored Empires'? . . . The idea is if we don't look out the white race will be—will be utterly submerged. It's all scientific stuff; it's been proved. . . . " Elsewhere, Tom reports that "it seems that pretty soon the earth's going to fall into the sun—or wait a minute—it's just the opposite—the sun's getting colder every year." Although there is "something pathetic" in Tom's ideas, his power is frighteningly lethal.

Jordan Baker is Daisy's double: they shared a similar "white girlhood" in their hometown. But Jordan does not seem nearly as feminine as Daisy: she throws her shoulders back "like a young cadet." She is a "new woman": she lives independently; unlike Daisy, she remains single; she has a professional life as a golfer. Though she is attractive to Nick, he fears that there is something "dishonest" about her, which is interesting considering the fact that she provides Nick with much of the background for the story. Like Nick, she acts as a liaison between Daisy and Gatsby.

Myrtle Wilson, Tom's mistress, offers an extreme contrast to Daisy. Whereas Daisy is inactive and wispy, Myrtle bursts with energy and vitality. She serves as a contrast to both the Buchanan's inherited wealth and Gatsby's acquired wealth: she lives above a garage and is pleased and easily bought with trinkets and baubles. In Myrtle, Fitzgerald sketches an interesting and problematic portrait of working-class vulgarity and heightened female sexuality. Ultimately, of course, Myrtle dies on the road, run down by the "death car."

George Wilson, Myrtle's husband, becomes Tom Buchanan's tool. He owns an automobile garage in the "valley of ashes"—an industrial wasteland between New York and West Egg. Although automobiles are everywhere in the novel, his economic position seems precarious. Wilson is pale, weak, and in poor health. As it dawns on him that his wife is having an affair, he dreams of taking her away to the country, and he foolishly appeals to Tom for help. When his wife is run down, he becomes desperate and violent. He shoots Gatsby to avenge his wife's death, and then kills himself.

Meyer Wolfshiem, Gatsby's business associate, is one of the men who "fixed the World Series"—a gangster. His cameo appearance paints a picture of Gatsby's connection to crime. His name plays on "wolf" and marks his Jewishness. He epitomizes the very things that Tom Buchanan apparently fears: the rising economic power of "racial others." In the case of Wolfshiem, the novel seems to agree with Buchanan: Nick condemns Wolfshiem's failure to display real friendship to Gatsby. ❀

Critical Views on
The Great Gatsby

MALCOLM COWLEY ON DIFFERENT FORMS OF WEALTH

[Malcolm Cowley (1898–1989) was an editor, critic, and award-winning writer. His books include *Exile's Return: A Literary Odyssey of the 1920s* and *A Second Flowering: Works and Days of the Lost Generation.* He also edited a collection of F. Scott Fitzgerald's short stories. In this essay, he reads *The Great Gatsby* as an allegory about America's changing economy during the 1920s.]

In his attitude toward money he revealed the new spirit of an age when conspicuous accumulation was giving way to conspicuous earning and spending. It was an age when gold was melted down and became fluid; when wealth was no longer measured in possessions—land, houses, livestock, machinery—but rather in dollars per year, as a stream is measured by its flow; when for the first time the expenses of government were being met by income taxes more than by property and excise taxes; and when the new tax structure was making it somewhat more difficult to accumulate a stable and lasting fortune. Such fortunes still existed at the hardly accessible peak of the social system, which young men dreamed of reaching like Alpinists, but the romantic figures of the age were not capitalists properly speaking. They were salaried executives and advertising men, they were promoters, salesmen, stock gamblers, or racketeers, and they were millionaires in a new sense—not men each of whom owned a million dollars' worth of property, but men who lived in rented apartments and had nothing but stock certificates and insurance policies (or nothing but credit and the right connections), while spending more than the income of the old millionaires.

The change went deep into the texture of American society and deep into the feelings of Americans as individuals. Fitzgerald is its most faithful recorder. ⟨ . . . ⟩

Nick stands for the older values that prevailed in the Midwest before the First World War. His family is not tremendously rich like the Buchanans, but it has a long-established and sufficient fortune, so that Nick is the only person in the book who has not been corrupted by seeking or spending money. He is so certain of his own values that he hesitates to criticize others, but when he does pass judgment—on Gatsby, on Jordan Baker, on the Buchanans—he speaks as for ages to come.

All the other characters belong to their own brief era of confused and dissolving standards, but they are affected by the era in different fashions. Each of them represents some particular variety of moral failure; Lionel Trilling says that they are "treated as if they were ideographs," a true observation; but the treatment does not detract from their reality as persons. Tom Buchanan is wealth brutalized by selfishness and arrogance; he looks for a mistress in the valley of ashes and finds an ignorant woman, Myrtle Wilson, whose raw vitality is like his own. Daisy Buchanan is the butterfly soul of wealth and offers a continual promise "that she had done gay, exciting things just a while since and that there were gay, exciting things hovering in the next hour"; but it is a false promise, since at heart she is as self-centered as Tom and even colder. Jordan Baker apparently lives by the old standards, but she uses them only as a subterfuge. Aware of her own cowardice and dishonesty, she feels "safer on a plane where any divergence from a code would be thought impossible."

All these except Myrtle Wilson are East Egg people, that is, they are part of a community where wealth takes the form of solid possessions. Set against them are the West Egg people, whose wealth is fluid income that might cease to flow. The West Egg people, with Gatsby as their tragic hero, have worked furiously to rise in the world, but they will never reach East Egg for all the money they spend; at most they can sit at the water's edge and look across the bay at the green light that shines and promises at the end of the Buchanan's dock.

—Malcolm Cowley, "Fitzgerald: The Romance of Money." In *Modern Critical Views: F. Scott Fitzgerald,* ed. Harold Bloom (New York: Chelsea House Publishers, 1985): pp. 63, 71.

ROBERT ORNSTEIN ON THE SYMBOLISM OF THE EAST AND THE WEST

[Robert Ornstein is Professor of English Literature at Case Western Reserve University, and is the author of *Moral Vision* in *Jacobean Tragedy* and *Kingdom for a Stage: The Achievement of Shakespeare's History Plays.* In this essay, he reads the novel as a fable that turns the myth of the American frontier backward upon itself, and makes the East the object of the American dream.]

Gatsby is a story of "displaced persons" who have journeyed eastward in search of a larger experience of life. ⟨ . . . ⟩ To Fitzgerald ⟨ . . . ⟩ the lure of the East represents a profound displacement of the American dream, a turning back upon itself of the historical pilgrimage towards the frontier which had, in fact, created and sustained that dream. In *Gatsby* the once limitless western horizon is circumscribed by the "bored, sprawling, swollen towns beyond the Ohio, with their interminable inquisitions which spared only the children and the very old." The virgin territories of the frontiersmen have been appropriated by the immigrant families, the diligent Swedes—the unimaginative, impoverished German families like Henry Gatz. Thus after a restless nomadic existence, the Buchanans settle "permanently" on Long Island because Tom would be a "God damned fool to live anywhere else." Thus Nick comes to New York with a dozen volumes on finance which promise "to unfold the shining secrets that only Midas, Morgan and Maecenas knew." Gatsby's green light, of course, shines in only one direction—from the East across the Continent to Minnesota, from the East across the bay to his imitation mansion in West Egg.

Lying in the moonlight on Gatsby's deserted beach, Nick realizes at the close just how lost a pilgrimage Gatsby's had been:

> . . . I became aware of the old island here that had flowered once for Dutch sailor's eyes—a fresh, green breast of the new world. Its vanished trees, the trees that had made way for Gatsby's house, had once pandered in whispers to the last and greatest of all human dreams; for a transitory moment man must have held his breath in the presence of this continent, compelled into an aesthetic contemplation he neither understood nor desired, face to face for the last time in history with something commensurate to his capacity for wonder.

Gatsby is the spiritual descendant of these Dutch sailors. Like them, he set out for gold and stumbled on a dream. But he journeys in the wrong direction in time as well as space. The transitory enchanted moment has come and gone for him and for the others, making the romantic promise of the future an illusory reflection of the past. ⟨ . . . ⟩

After Gatsby's death Nick prepares to return to his Minnesota home, a place of warmth and enduring stability, carrying with him a surrealistic night vision of the debauchery of the East. Yet his return is not a positive rediscovery of the well-springs of American life. Instead it seems a melancholy retreat from the ruined promise of the East, from the empty present to the childhood memory of the past. Indeed, it is this childhood memory, not the reality of the West which Nick cherishes. For he still thinks the East, despite its nightmarish aspect, superior to the stultifying small-town dullness from which he fled. And by the close of *Gatsby* it is unmistakably clear that the East does not symbolize the contemporary decadence and the West the pristine virtues of an earlier America. Fitzgerald does not contrast Gatsby's criminality with his father's unspoiled rustic strength and dignity. He contrasts rather Henry Gatz's dull, grey, almost insentient existence, "a meaningless extinction up an alley," with Gatsby's pilgrimage Eastward, which, though hopeless and corrupting, was at least a journey of life and hope—an escape from the "vast obscurity" of the West that once spawned and then swallowed the American dream. Into this vast obscurity the Buchanans finally disappear.

—Robert Ornstein, "Scott Fitzgerald's Fable of East and West" In *Modern Critical Views: F. Scott Fitzgerald,* ed. Harold Bloom (New York: Chelsea House, 1985): pp. 75–76, 78.

Marius Bewley on the Two Levels of Daisy Buchanan

[Marius Bewley (1918–1973) was a prolific literary critic and Professor of American Literature at Rutgers University. His books include *The Eccentric Design* (1957) and *Masks and Mirrors: Essays in Criticism* (1970). In this excerpt, he analyzes the role of Daisy in *The Great Gatsby*.]

Daisy Buchanan exists at two well-defined levels in the novel. She is what she is—but she exists at the level of Gatsby's vision of her. Even Fitzgerald's admirers regard Daisy as rather a good, if somewhat silly, little thing; but Fitzgerald knew that at its most depraved levels the American dream merges with the American debutante's dream—a thing of deathly hollowness. Fitzgerald faces up squarely to the problem of telling us what Daisy has to offer in a human relationship. At one of Gatsby's fabulous parties—the one to which Daisy brings her husband, Tom Buchanan—Gatsby points out to Daisy and Tom, among the celebrated guests, one particular couple:

> 'Perhaps you know that lady,' Gatsby indicated a gorgeous, scarcely human orchid of a woman who sat in state under a white-plum tree. Tom and Daisy stared, with that peculiarly unreal feeling that accompanies the recognition of a hitherto ghostly celebrity of the movies.
> 'She's lovely,' said Daisy.
> 'That man bending over her is her director.' 〈 . . . 〉

Daisy likes the moving-picture actress because she has no substance. She is a gesture that is committed to nothing more real than her own image on the silver screen. She has become a gesture divorced forever from the tiresomeness of human reality. In effect, this passage is Daisy's confession of faith. She virtually announces here what her criteria of human emotions and conduct are. Fitzgerald's illustration of the emptiness of Daisy's character—an emptiness that we see curdling into the viciousness of a monstrous moral indifference as the story unfolds—is drawn with a fineness and depth of critical understanding, and communicated with a force of imagery so rare in modern American writing, that it is almost astonishing that he is often credited with giving in to those very qualities which *The Great Gatsby* so effectively excoriates.

But what is the basis for the mutual attraction between Daisy and Gatsby? In Daisy's case the answer is simple. We remember that Nick Carraway has described Gatsby's personality as an 'unbroken series of successful gestures'. Superficially, Daisy finds in Gatsby, or thinks she finds, that safety from human reality which the empty gesture implies. What she fails to realize is that Gatsby's gorgeous gesturings are the reflex of an aspiration towards the possibilities of life, and this is something entirely different from those vacant images of romance and sophistication that fade so easily into the nothingness from which they came. But in a sense, Daisy is safe enough from the reality she dreads. The true question is not what Gatsby sees in Daisy, but the direction he takes from her, what he sees *beyond* her; and that has, despite the immaturity intrinsic in Gatsby's vision, an element of grandeur in it. For Gatsby, Daisy does not exist in herself. She is the green light that signals him into the heart of his ultimate vision. *Why* she should have this evocative power over Gatsby is a question Fitzgerald faces beautifully and successfully as he recreates that milieu of uncritical snobbishness and frustrated idealism—monstrous fusion—which is the world in which Gatsby is compelled to live. ⟨ . . . ⟩

Daisy's significance in the story lies in her failure to constitute the objective correlative of Gatsby's vision. And at the same time, Daisy's wonderfully representative quality as a creature of the Jazz Age relates her personal failure to the larger failure of Gatsby's society to satisfy his need. In fact, Fitzgerald never allows Daisy's failure to become a human or personal one. He maintains it with sureness on a symbolic level where it is identified with and reflects the failure of Gatsby's decadent American world.

—Marius Bewley, "Scott Fitzgerald and the Collapse of the American Dream." In *Modern Critical Views: F. Scott Fitzgerald,* ed. Harold Bloom (New York: Chelsea House Publishers, 1985): pp. 38–40.

Henry Dan Piper on the Odor of Mortality

[Henry Dan Piper is the author of *F. Scott Fitzgerald: A Critical Portrait* and a distinguished educator. In this essay, he explores the themes of death and the symbol of J. T. Eckleburg in *The Great Gatsby.*]

Nick, unlike Gatsby, is continually aware of the fact that man must die. Indeed the odor of mortality is everywhere in the novel, even more in the early drafts than in the published version of the text. In one draft, when Gatsby proudly shows Nick his oversized yellow sports car ("the death car," as the New York newspapers will later call it after Myrtle's death), Nick is automatically reminded of a hearse. Indeed, a few paragraphs further on, when Nick is riding in Gatsby's car to New York, he actually passes a funeral and is confronted with the image of "a dead man . . . in a hearse heaped full of flowers." Undoubtedly the most conspicuous death image in the novel is that of the waste land of dust and ashes over which Gatsby and his neighbors must pass every time they go to New York. ⟨ . . . ⟩

Over this portentous waste land brood the sightless eyes of Dr. T. J. Eckleburg—rooted (as Fitzgerald says in another deleted passage) "in a spot that reeks of death." Nearby stands the squalid, ash-covered garage of George Wilson, the insane agent of Gatsby's doom. ⟨ . . . ⟩

At the end, the simple fact of Gatsby's death is quickly stated in a sentence. But the implications of that death necessitate a long, concluding chapter. No one besides Nick is willing to confront those implications. Gatsby's fatuous father, (an obvious contrast to Nick's father) consoles himself with the sordid lie of his dead son's "success." Gatsby's other friends all stay away presumably following the corrupt Wolfshiem's maxim that in matters connected with death "it is better to leave everything alone." Only Nick is incapable of letting things alone. The fact of his neighbor's death rouses Nick—the hitherto passive onlooker—to one of the few positive actions of his career. ⟨ . . . ⟩

Nick's vicarious involvement in Gatsby's destiny, in other words, has permitted him to see the world for a brief space through the glasses of Dr. T. J. Eckleburg. What he sees is a waste land without moral sanctions of any kind, an anarchy in which romantic idealists like Gatsby are the most vulnerable of all. "After Gatsby's death," Nick says, "the East was haunted for me . . . distorted beyond my eyes' power of correction. So . . . I decided to come back home." Dr. Eckleburg is the symbol of a world without the idea of God, a kind of anti-God. When George Wilson discovers that his wife has been unfaithful he drags her to the window of his garage and there, in front of the eyes of Dr. Eckleburg, tells her: "God knows what you've been doing. You may fool me but you can't fool God." "God sees everything," the vengeance-crazed husband tells Michaelis after Myrtle's death, just before setting off on his quest for vengeance. As we might expect, he only succeeds in killing the wrong man.

—Henry Dan Piper, "The Untrimmed Christmas Tree: The Religious Background of *The Great Gatsby*." In *The Great Gatsby: A Study*, ed. Frederick J. Hoffman (New York: Charles Scribner's Sons, 1962): pp. 331–333.

[Leo Marx is the author of *The Machine in the Garden: Technology and the Pastoral Ideal in America.* He is also a distinguished educator, having taught at Massachusetts Institute of Technology and Amherst College. In this excerpt the author evaluates the differences between Nick's and Gatsby's attitudes toward nature and the pastoral ideal.]

Gatsby's tragic career exemplifies the attenuation of the pastoral ideal in America. In the beginning Nick compares Gatsby's "heightened sensitivity to the promises of life" to a seismograph—a delicate instrument peculiarly responsive to invisible signals emanating from the land. Gatsby's entire existence—not only the "romantic readiness" of his spirit, but also his Horatio Alger rise to affluence—had been shaped by the special conditions of which the bountiful, green landscape is the token. Young James Gatz got his start by using his intimate knowledge of the Midwestern terrain to save a rich man's yacht. It was at that moment that Jay Gatsby sprang, like a son of God, from his Platonic conception of himself. The incident, a turning point in his life, marks the enlistment of native energies in the service of wealth, status, power, and, as Nick puts it, of "a vast, vulgar and meretricious beauty." Nick, the real hero of *The Great Gatsby,* is the only one, finally, to understand, but it takes him a long while to grasp the subtle interplay between Gatsby's dream and his underworld life. ⟨ . . . ⟩

The difference between Gatsby's point of view and Nick's illustrates the distinction, with which I began, between sentimental and complex pastoralism. Fitzgerald, through Nick, expresses a point of view typical of a great many twentieth-century American writers. The work of Faulkner, Frost, Hemingway and West comes to mind. Again and again they invoke the image of a green landscape—a terrain either wild or, if cultivated, rural—as a symbolic repository of meaning and value. But at the same time they acknowledge the power of a counterforce, a machine or some other symbol of the forces which have stripped the old ideal of most, if not all, of its meaning. Complex pastoralism, to put it another way, acknowledges the reality of history. One of Nick Carraway's great moments of illumination occurs when he realizes that Gatsby wants nothing less of Daisy than that she should go to Tom, and say, "'I never loved you.'" And when Nick objects, observing that one cannot undo the past, Gatsby is incredulous. Of course he can. "'I'm going to fix everything,'" he says, "'just the way it was before. ...'" Like Melville's Starbuck, Gatsby would let faith oust fact. He is another example of the modern primitive described by Ortega, the industrial *Naturmensch* who is blind to the complexity of modern civilization; he wants his automobile, enjoys it, yet regards it as "the spontaneous fruit of an Edenic tree." Nick also is drawn to images of pastoral felicity, but he learns how destructive they are when cherished in lieu of reality. He realizes that Gatsby is destroyed by his inability to distinguish between dreams and facts. In the characteristic pattern of complex pastoralism, the fantasy of pleasure is checked by the facts of history.

> —Leo Marx, *The Machine in the Garden: Technology and the Pastoral Ideal in America.* In *F. Scott Fitzgerald: Critical Assessments,* vol. II, ed. Henry Claridge (East Sussex, England: Helm Information, 1991): pp. 304–305.

DAVID PARKER ON TWO VERSIONS OF THE HERO

[David Parker has taught English at the University of Malaya and is the author of *Ethics, Theory and the Novel.* He has also published essays on Chaucer and Shakespeare. In this essay, he compares *The Great Gatsby* to Browning's *Childe Rolande,* identifying the two heroic ideals in the novel: Gatsby is a typical romantic quest hero, while Nick is a hero of sentimental education.]

There are in English literature two chief versions of the hero. Often they share characteristics, and sometimes a hero is a blend of the two, but there is a tendency for polarisation in one direction or the other, towards distinct patterns of behaviour and character. The first kind of hero is the one whose prototype we find in mediaeval romance and ancient epic: an idealist, loyal to some transcending object, and relentless in his quest for it. He seeks honour, love, or the Sangreal, and he affects the reader with all the potency of myth. The second kind, though doubtless developed from the first, is in sharp contrast. If he has a quest, it is essentially an inward one. Circumstances compel him to explore his own being, to discover, and perhaps to modify, his own identity. He is typified by the hero of the novel of sentimental education. ⟨ ... ⟩

Another difference between the two sorts of hero is in what they recognize as real. Nick and Gatsby see different realities. Gatsby's is naturally that of the hero of romance. The everyday is unreal for him; reality is what he has discovered through his dreams. The hero of the novel of sentimental education lives in a world where reality is elusive: he thinks he possesses it, but finally discovers it only when his education is completed. The hero of romance, on the other hand, is from the beginning acquainted with reality, though he may have to wait to possess it, as Childe Roland has to wait for the Dark Tower. Heredity makes Gatsby a dreamer. His father, whom we meet only after the son's death, like Gatsby prefers the image to the object. He sets more value on an old and cherished photograph of Gatsby's mansion than on the mansion itself. 'He had shown it so often', remarks Nick, 'that I think it was more real to him now than the house itself'. There is irony in Gatsby's dying at the hand of just such another dreamer, Wilson who projects a dream of divine providence onto the massive eyes of Doctor T. J. Eckleburg watching over the valley of ashes.

Gatsby's apprehension of reality is explained in a much quoted passage:

> The truth was that Jay Gatsby of West Egg, Long Island, sprang from his Platonic conception of himself. He was a son of God—a phrase which, if it means anything, means just that—and he must be about His Father's business, the service of a vast, vulgar, and meretricious beauty. So he invented just the sort of Jay Gatsby that a seventeen-year-old boy would be likely to invent, and to this conception he was faithful to the end.

Gatsby touches all his surroundings with this gaudy idealism, in an effort to persuade himself of the 'unreality of reality'. Owl-eyes, the sympathetic drunk inexplicably adrift in Gatsby's world, marvels that the books in his library are real—not 'nice durable cardboard'—and compares Gatsby to Belasco, the producer noted for his insistence on authentic properties. Like Belasco, Gatsby is more of a showman than an artist, but he puts his heart into the show. Daisy could not but fall short of Gatsby's dream, Nick points out: 'It had gone beyond her, beyond everything. He had thrown himself into it with creative passion, adding to it all the time, decking it out with every bright feather that drifted his way. No amount of fire or freshness can challenge what a man can store up in his ghostly heart'.

—David Parker, "*The Great Gatsby:* Two Versions of the Hero" In *Modern Critical Views: F. Scott Fitzgerald,* ed. Harold Bloom (New York: Chelsea House, 1985): pp. 141–142, 153–154.

[In this extract, Ron Neuhaus identifies Fitzgerald's paradoxical and unsuccessful creation of Nick Carraway as a simultaneously first-person and omniscient narrator.]

Fitzgerald himself was keenly aware that *Gatsby* was a flawed work but the nature and origin of its major flaws escaped him. In a frank letter to Edmund Wilson in 1925, he explained what he takes to be the novel's "BIG FAULT."

> I gave no account of (and had no feeling about or knowledge of) the emotional relationship between Gatsby and Daisy from the time of their reunion to the catastrophe.

But his inability to handle relations between Gatsby and Daisy is merely symptomatic of more crucial faults in the novel: that of a breakdown in narrative technique, and an inability to create fully fleshed characters beneath the "blankets of excellent prose" Fitzgerald refers to later in the letter. *Gatsby* begins with first person narration, but Fitzgerald will not accept the limitation of this self-imposed restriction and constantly strains toward an "omniscient *I*" though diction, flashback, and reconstructed events. Despite his ingenuity, he fails to create a responsible fiction. He finds the first person perspective inadequate for the credibility of his moral stance, yet he will not take the responsibility involved with an omniscient perspective. The first person limitation enables him to avoid the scenes (as he notes in his letter) that his insights could not handle. Nick literally chaperones what could be scenes of revealing intimacy between Gatsby and Daisy.

Another factor, not stylistic but of strong influence, was the cultural climate of the post-war decade. The problems of character and style reflect a mood in which a desire for moral security remained ("the world to be in uniform and at a sort of moral attention," as Nick says), but found itself in a world which could not provide that fulfillment. The moral authority of first person narrative was not adequate for such a context, and Fitzgerald tried to create esthetically what could not be discovered naturally. To this end, he experimented with multiple perspective. The efforts at extending perspective are admirable enough: the later movement into Gatsby's and Daisy's minds, into Michaelis' account of the car accident, as well as the intimate details of Gatsby's past—but through the early extended use of first person Fitzgerald has painted himself into a corner. As point of view makes some blatant shifts late in the novel, there is no sense of multiple perspective or modulation, but rather of an attempt to maintain, however thinly, the moral perspective of the first person narration, while at the same time trying to bring in the third person credibility. The reader has a collection of fragments, conceivably from different perspectives, but what differentiates Fitzgerald from Pound, Eliot, Joyce, or Faulkner in his later work is that they did not structure their respective works around a solitary informing consciousness.

—Ron Neuhaus, "*Gatsby* and the Failure of the Omniscient 'I'." In *F. Scott Fitzgerald: Critical Assessments,* vol. II, ed. Henry Claridge (East Sussex, England: Helm Information, 1991): pp. 359–360.

KEATH FRASER ON A "MAN'S BOOK"

[Keath Fraser is the author of *As For Me and My Body: A Memoir of Sinclair Ross* and *Taking Cover.* In this essay, he argues that Fitzgerald created a world of "sexual anarchy" in *The Great Gatsby,* drawing attention to the fact that the novel is primarily interested in men, male bodies, and male relationships.]

Writing to Maxwell Perkins before publication of his novel, Fitzgerald confessed that "it may hurt the book's popularity that it's a *man's book.*" By this he meant that his best characters were men and that his women faded out of the novel. In the same letter Fitzgerald had to agree with his editor that until now he had not revealed enough about Gatsby—which would allow Gatsby, and not Tom Buchanan, to dominate his story. Throughout the novel Nick holds the masculine forms of Gatsby and Tom in sharp contrast. For him, Gatsby's form seems preferable to Tom's, yet it is Tom's masculinity which captures Nick's attention in so convincing a manner that critics of the novel, in identifying the grander theme of the American dream, have perceived in Tom the cruel and palpable foil to Gatsby's idealism and illusion. For Nick the "gorgeous" Gatsby fails to come "alive" until Jordan Baker explains to him that Gatsby's house was deliberately chosen by its owner to be across the bay from Daisy's own house in East Egg. Then, says Nick, "He came alive to me, delivered suddenly from the womb of his purposeless splendor." In contrast to the insuperably *physical* purpose in the novel of Tom Buchanan, Gatsby and his purpose seem clearly metaphysical, springing agilely from that "platonic conception of himself." Imagery associated with Gatsby suggests solipsism, sexlessness. It is otherwise with Tom: "Not even the effeminate swank of his riding clothes," Nick observes, "could hide the enormous power of that body—he seemed to fill those glistening boots until he strained the top lacing, and you could see a great pack of muscle shifting when his shoulder moved under his thin coat. It was a body capable of enormous leverage—a cruel body."

Here is a body of rather more interest to Nick than the one he courts in Jordan Baker. In fact, it fascinates him. As the novel progresses Tom's body comes to represent, far more than Gatsby's corruption and criminal associates do, the threat and evil force of the book. ⟨T⟩he scene which follows between Tom and Wilson at the garage ⟨underscores⟩ the underlying competition between the two rivals for Myrtle Wilson's favours. ⟨ . . . ⟩

⟨T⟩he sexual undertow adrift in the particular images which link Wilson and Tom has been carefully set up by Fitzgerald to contrast the two male rivals. ⟨ . . . ⟩

If it is the lover which intrigues Nick in Gatsby, it is the *man* which intrigues him in Tom; our failure to notice the delicate way in which Fitzgerald allows Nick to perceive Tom's relationship with Wilson has limited our response to the full play of sexuality in the story. Fitzgerald, by letting Nick have the kind of reverberating observations he does—observations increasingly integral to the way his narrator comes to look at the world—creates a kind of sexual anarchy in *The Great Gatsby.* It is a narrative of potency and impotency, of jealous sex and Platonic love, of sexuality, in fact, owing more to simultaneity of withinness and withoutness than the narrator appears to be aware of confessing.

—Keath Fraser, "Another Reading of *The Great Gatsby*," *English Studies in Canada* 5, no. 3 (Fall 1979): pp. 335–338.

Irving S. Saposnik on the Car and Car Culture

[Irving S. Saposnik is Professor at the University of Wisconsin and author of *Robert Louis Stevenson*. In this essay, he explores the various metaphorical meanings of the automobile in the novel.]

⟨A⟩s object and metaphor the automobile pervades the moral and emotional texture of the novel. Its value is rarely neutral, yet it is never the same in the hands of all: for Nick, his Dodge is as commonplace as his dog and his Finnish cleaning lady; for Daisy, her white roadster is a symbol of a lost girlhood now as irretrievable as the pearls she wore on her wedding day; and for Gatsby, his "gorgeous car" with "three noted horn" is his wonder horse, upon which he can make his gallant entrance "balancing himself on the dashboard" as if he were really a cowboy hero. Gatsby's guests, that uninvited mob that invades his house as if it were an amusement park, similarly, are borne by the automobile in such numbers that its very presence, "five-deep in the drive," testifies to their rite of passage. As much as Nick may associate his Midwest with the thrilling returning trains of his youth, his East is visualized as "the constant flicker of men and women and machines," "the throbbing taxicabs," the view from the Queensboro Bridge at sunset in which the city is always seen for the first time, "in its first wild promise of all the mystery and beauty in the world."

On the one hand the car is a new god, a Pegasus that "With fenders spread like wings" scatters light as it races along the highway; on the other hand it is the "death car" that cuts down Myrtle Wilson even as she prepares to escape from her ashen home. Morally ambivalent, it becomes in the Twenties not only a universal means of escape, but the great vehicle of physical and social mobility. The *Gatsby* society seems to be in constant motion, driving to and from the city across a landscape that is dominated not only by the valley of ashes but also by roadhouse roofs and "wayside garages, where new red gas-pumps sat out in pools of light. . . . " These all become part of the modern scene and are as natural to the eye as Doctor Eckleburg's massive billboard that is also a product of the new car culture. ⟨ . . . ⟩

⟨N⟩ot only the car but the car culture serves as a vehicle that lures all the characters, particularly Gatsby, to pursue a never-ending dream. ⟨ . . . ⟩

The car is everyone's dream in this first great automotive age, and it appears throughout *Gatsby* as a source of both admiration and aspiration. When Nick and Gatsby drive into the city in Gatsby's "circus wagon," they are viewed by two sets of socially-mobile Americans: a group of Southern-Europeans for whom Gatsby's car represents wonderful possibility; and "three modish negroes, two bucks and a girl," whose limousine and white chauffeur proclaim their "haughty rivalry." The car plays a dominant role in *Gatsby* commensurate with its prominent position in American culture where, as Daniel Boorstin observes, "The automobile has been the great vehicle of American civilization in the Twentieth Century. Seldom has a people found in technology so appropriate, so versatile, and so pervasive an expression."

> —Irving S. Saposnik, *The Passion and the Life: Technology as Pattern in The Great Gatsby* (Detroit: Bruccoli Clark, 1980): pp. 183, 185.

SUSAN RESNECK PARR ON THE SEARCH FOR ORDER

[Susan Resneck Parr has served as the Dean of the College of Arts and Sciences at the University of Tulsa and is the author of *The Moral of the Story: Literature, Values, and American Education*. In this excerpt, she argues that Gatsby dramatizes the human search for order in the face of flux, change, and the passage of time.]

Nick especially seems to need a sense of order. After his experiences during World War I, he decides that "instead of being the warm centre of the world, the Middle West now seemed like the ragged edge of the universe." His response to such feelings of disorientation are to choose the path that "everybody I knew" had chosen: moving to New York and entering the bond business. The choice is without risk, for both his aunts and uncles concur with it, and his father agrees to support him for a year.

Nick, however, becomes increasingly unsettled as events force him to move beyond thoughts about life's promise and bring him face to face with its harsher realities. For example, when he learns of Tom's affair with Myrtle, he feels "confused and a little disgusted." He also assumes that Daisy will share his reaction, observing, "It seemed to me that the thing for Daisy to do was to rush out of the house, child in arms." When Myrtle's sister tells him that Daisy won't give Tom a divorce because she is Catholic, Nick is "a little shocked at the elaborateness of the lie." ⟨ . . . ⟩

After the scene in the Plaza, when Daisy, Gatsby, and Tom display such raw emotion, Nick reacts even more intensely. Now he is explicit that he sees change as being not exciting but dangerous. Shed of his own illusions about Gatsby's past and also about Daisy's ability to be worthy of Gatsby's dream, Nick remembers that the day marks his thirtieth birthday and thinks, "Before me stretched the portentous, menacing road of a new decade."

Such negative feelings prompt Nick to decide that "human sympathy has its limits." As Tom drives Nick and Jordan back to East Egg, Nick feels remote from Tom and from his heightened emotions. For the moment at least, he turns to Jordan, who, "unlike Daisy, was too wise ever to carry well-forgotten dreams from age to age." He also continues to think of the future as threatening, not exciting. ⟨ . . . ⟩

The night of Myrtle's death, Nick cannot sleep because, as he tells it, "I tossed half-sick between grotesque reality and savage, frightening dreams." In other words, neither reality unadorned by illusion nor illusion itself offers an escape from feelings of vulnerability. Soon, however, Nick decides that it is the East that is "haunted" for him, "distorted beyond my eyes' power of correction." In his mind, West Egg is especially disturbing. It remains in his "more fantastic dreams" as "a night scene by El Greco"— "grotesque, crouching under a sullen, overhanging sky and a lustreless moon" in which wealth is irrelevant in the face of the lack of order and caring.

To escape this world where reality is grotesque and where even nature is not nurturing but threatening, Nick decides to go home again. ⟨ . . . ⟩ Not unexpectedly, his need for order persists. Even though he has come to think that he may be "half in love" with Jordan, he ends their relationship because he "wanted to leave things in order and not just trust that obliging and indifferent sea to sweep my refuse away." Nick is also explicit that he no longer wants complexity or to be a "well-rounded man"; instead, he has decided that "life is much more successfully looked at from a single window after all."

—Susan Resneck Parr, "The Idea of Order at West Egg," *New Essays on The Great Gatsby*, ed. Matthew J. Bruccoli (Cambridge: Cambridge University Press, 1985): pp. 73–75.

MICHAEL HOLQUIST ON THE OXYMORON

[Michael Holquist is the author of *Dostoevsky and the Novel* with Katerina Clark and Mikhail Bakhtin. He is Professor of Comparative and Slavic Literature at Yale University. In this essay, he argues that *The Great Gatsby's* representations of identity, character, and subjectivity are structured by the rhetorical trope of the oxymoron (a combination of incongruous words).]

While the main body of the narrative is compressed in time to a few months in 1922 and in space to a small area of the east coast, this time/space is complicated both by its own pastness and thereness to the moment of its being put into writing by Nick, and by the pastness and thereness of the major characters prior to the events of 1922. In each case the relation of here and now to then and there is enacted as an incongruity, a discordance modeled in the constant inadequacy and breakdown of stereotypes.

The ambivalence and lack that characterize the stereotype are manifest in the novel as a complex series of contradictions and incommensurabilities. There are so very many of these and they are of such a variety, it may be said that the text is governed by the trope of oxymoron. It is first of all the most characteristic feature of Nick's narrative voice; the novel contains page after page of locutions such as I was "that most limited of all specialists, the 'well-rounded man'"; "the rock of the world was founded securely on a fairy's wing"; the First World War (which is, of course called "the great war") is a "delayed Teutonic migration", ceilings have "Presbyterian nymphs" on them, and characters eat their food with "ferocious delicacy." But the oxymoronic nature of the narrator's epigrams and descriptions is not merely stylistic. A dramatized incongruity characterizes virtually every aspect of the text. The title of *The Great Gatsby* is itself an oxymoron, an eponymous gap between its honorific adjective and the proper name of the sentimental gangster. Incongruity is at work in the novel's most obvious and superficial thematic level, the gap between Gatsby's image—his stereotype—of Daisy and Daisy as she is outside Gatsby's "riotous dream" of her as quest object. Incompatibility legislates the novel's basic narrative pattern, which is articulated as a rupture between events as they unfold in 1922 and Nick's act of chronicling the same events two years later. This break between event and representation as present disfigures all attempts in the novel to make past and present cohere, as in the gap between the point in 1917 in Louisville when Gatsby and Daisy first meet and the struggle each undertakes to continue that moment when they encounter each other on Long Island five years later. A grotesque incommensurability is a dominant of all the incidental features of the narrative as well, such as a vagrant selling stray dogs on the streets of Manhattan whose name is Rockefeller. This incommensurability is particularly bizarre in its mapping of America: when asked what part of the middle west he is from, a character replies, "San Francisco." ⟨ . . . ⟩

The oppositions are too obvious to dwell on. More often than not in the critical literature they have been treated at a characterological or psychologistic level, strategies that obscure the implications of such programmatically precise binarization for the process of subject formation. Subject formation not just for this or that individual actor in the novel but at the non-trivial level where it is a problem in the kind of representation that language will permit.

—Michael Holquist, "The Inevitability of Stereotype: Colonialism in *The Great Gatsby*." In *The Rhetoric of Interpretation and the Interpretation of Rhetoric,* ed. Paul Hernadi (Durham, N.C.: Duke University Press, 1989): pp. 211–213.

RICHARD LEHAN ON ALLUSIONS TO *THE WASTE LAND*

[Richard Lehan is Professor of English at the University of California, Los Angeles. He is the author of *F. Scott Fitzgerald and the Craft of Fiction.* In this excerpt, he describes the various landscapes in *The Great Gatsby,* and compares Fitzgerald's valley of ashes to T. S. Eliot's representation of landscape in his 1922 poem *The Waste Land.*]

Three settings dominate *The Great Gatsby,* and they descend metaphorically from the resplendent Georgian mansion of Tom Buchanan at East Egg to the luxurious but déclassé Normandy castle of Gatsby among the arrivistes of West Egg to the valley of ashes through which one has to pass in order to reach the city where one can find the high rich in the Plaza Hotel, the Wolfsheims and Buchanans at lunch in their Manhattan coves, and the apartment at 158th Street that Tom keeps for his lovemaking with Myrtle Wilson. Each of these settings takes on a symbolic meaning of its own, ending with the hell of the middle class, figured in the men with spades who work on the top of the ash mounds. Tom's mansion embodies the taste that established money knows how to buy. Impressive in its gaudy way, Gatsby's house is to Nick more like a world's fair, a place where the rules of conduct are more appropriate to an amusement park than a sedate residence of the established rich. 〈 . . . 〉

〈T〉he principal residents of the valley of ashes are George and Myrtle Wilson. They are really two sides of the same social coin: Myrtle still has "vitality about her as if the nerves of her body were continually smouldering," an image that is appropriate to her place in the valley of ashes. George, on the other hand, is already beaten down by life, has long since lost anything like vitality, and is described by Nick as an "anaemic" and "spiritless man" whom people walk around "as if he were a ghost." And ghost he is, similar to the walking dead that populate T. S. Eliot's *The Waste Land,* which Fitzgerald knew by heart.

A number of critics have connected *The Great Gatsby* and *The Waste Land.* The similarities cry out for attention. Like *The Waste Land,* *Gatsby* moves between and among people of different classes, like the upper class neurasthenic lady in her boudoir, the women discussing marriage and abortion in the pub, and the woman in her flat awaiting the sexual visit of the young man carbuncular. *The Waste Land* is also set against an urban background. 〈 . . . 〉

The Waste Land was Eliot's response to a postwar Europe experiencing radical change. Historically, one empire after another had fallen, the last being the Hapsburgs, with Great Britain in line to be the next "falling tower." Eliot depicts a world coming morally apart, a world that has no principle to hold it together. We see the rich with nerves on end; middle-class housewives caught entrapped in sterile and purposeless lives; and lower-class clerks seeking mere gratification, no matter how mechanical or unfulfilling. ⟨ . . . ⟩

Man had lost his primitive energy, had lost the basis for the Fisher King whose sacrificial vitality had been handed down in the form of Osiris, Adonis, Atiz, Tamuz, to Christ. Their vitality was now being played out, exhausted, in the post-Enlightenment world of science and technology. ⟨ . . . ⟩

This sense of the exhaustion of romantic possibility was inseparable from the postwar sense of world weariness that we find in both the story that Nick Carraway tells and in the story Tiresias tells in *The Waste Land.*

—Richard Lehan, *The Great Gatsby: The Limits of Wonder* (Boston: Twayne Publishers, 1990): pp. 91–95.

MITCHELL BREITWIESER ON *GATSBY* AS A STATEMENT OF AMERICA

[Mitchell Breitwieser is professor of English at the University of California, Berkeley. He is the author of *American Puritanism and the Defense of Mourning: Religion, Grief, and Ethnology in Mary White Rowlandson's Captivity Narrative.* In this essay, he articulates *Gatsby*'s challenge to American tradition and its celebration of the nation's underappreciated potential resources, both aesthetic and human: immigrants, the poor, jazz music.]

Fitzgerald's task in *The Great Gatsby* is to envision and then to preserve the image of a machine that can avail itself of the total range of American materials, discovering and bringing to perfection the implicit energies of a social whole. Such a perfect cyborg would remedy the various collapses and disillusionments of the post-war period by figuring its predecessor-machines as imperfect adumbrations of itself, rightly-minded but marred by pointless phobias, failures to recognize the potentialities of everything. Overhasty in their several dismissals of ready resources, the predecessors had hastily and foolishly discarded as waste much that was hardly used at all, and succumbed to depression when confronted with the magnitude of a world that did not correspond to their designs. . . . ⟨T⟩he Gatsby machine invites everyone to the brightest party, thereby righting the American machine, putting it back on the road: "It was a rich cream color, bright with nickel, swollen here and there in its monstrous length with triumphant hat-boxes and supper-boxes and tool-boxes, and terraced with a labyrinth of wind-shields that mirrored a dozen suns. Sitting down between many layers of glass in a sort of green leather conservatory, we started to town." American culture, Fitzgerald suggests, is depleted after Woodrow Wilson and World War I, because, in its insistence on being high-toned, it has prematurely discarded a great deal of voltage. Nervously skirting its discards, it has failed to see that the reserve has barely been touched. Gatsby himself, for instance, pulsing with the energies of "the hot struggles of the poor": "There was, after all, something gorgeous about him, some heightened sensitivity to life that you might expect in some race as yet unborn." Fitzgerald raises the question of the remains, therefore, not to vilify the exploitiveness of America, or to mourn a lost America, but to argue that the moral America that burned dim in Woodrow Wilson, depressed by its mess, had failed to apprehend the calorie-count of what it considered burned out and tried not to see. Guiltily avoiding its discards, moral America blinded itself to a continent of energy-potency—Jewish gangsters, gambling, liquor, blue-collar boys, backseat sex, the Id, as it was called then, and jazz. As denizens of the novel's worldview, we are to be unaffected, bemused, a little repulsed by Tom Buchanan's fear of the world's dark people not because it is racist but because it would allow so much energy to go its own way. ⟨ . . . ⟩

The Great Gatsby may be, for all of its preemptive melancholy, the major statement of America realized as world-power and imperial presence, as ideologically crucial in its day as Franklin's *Autobiography* had been in its. (The debt is explicitly acknowledged in the account of Gatsby's boyhood.) Both books promote an ingenious and alert vigilance that diagnoses its predecessor's dispiritedness as a symptom of its failure to recognize the opportunity waiting ready in the surrounding actual world: sensations of alienation and exhaustion result from an overnarrow understanding of the extent to which the world can respond to design is only sufficiently capacious, can answer, that is, an ingenious and open summons to exploitation. Both books open the question of the predecessor's nightmare—its real, its occluded sociality—not as an inquiry into cultural heterogeneity but as a prolegomenon to the construction of a society utterly responsive to unification by a single design.

—Mitchell Breitwieser, "*The Great Gatsby:* Grief, Jazz, and the Eye-Witness," *Arizona Quarterly* 47, no. 3 (Autumn 1991): pp. 36–40.

DAVID L. MINTER ON GATSBY'S FAILURE

[David L. Minter is professor of English at Rice University. He is the author of *A Cultural History of the American Novel: Henry James to William Faulkner.* In this extract, he discusses how Jay Gatsby fails in his attempt to build a perfect life in a perfect world.]

The Great Gatsby is permeated with corruption and contains, in the valley of ashes, Fitzgerald's starkest image of the new world as waste land, yet it is not in the end simply a grim story. Jay Gatsby's "incorruptible" version of the "last and greatest of all human dreams"—the dream of building a new and perfect life in a new and perfect world—serves, as several critics have noted, to relieve the novel's grimness, to recast its bleakness. Gatsby's action—his building, both as activity and as artifact—ends, however, in "huge incoherent failure," not in success. It serves accordingly rather to make relief possible than in itself to represent relief. The whole of Gatsby's story, including both his dream and his absurd plan for realizing it—his plan for procuring a fortune, a mansion, and a bride—is redeemed from corruption and waste, from failure and absurdity only through Nick Carraway's effort imaginatively to interpret and render it. ⟨ . . . ⟩

Behind Gatsby there is a history of dislocation and alienation, the attendants, as it were, of the experience of immigration, and thus of the very process of Americanization. But behind him there also is an imagined history. On one side, he is James Gatz, the son of "shiftless and unsuccessful farm people." On the other, he is Jay Gatsby, the child of "his Platonic conception of himself," the heir to a history almost wholly "invented." Unable in the presence of abundance, of mansions in the town and yachts upon the lake, to accept dislocation and deprivation, his imagination has created an identity, a "conception," to which he remains "faithful to the end."

James Gatz's attempt to become Jay Gatsby, his attempt to live out of his invented history, entails an attempt to realize his "unutterable" dream. Given his world, his dream, despite its "gaudiness," is necessary. At times its vitality almost overwhelms him, almost reduces him to a mere embodiment of its impulse; and at times he almost fatally betrays it by making devotion to it take the form of service to a beauty that is "vast, vulgar, and meretricious." From outset to end, he just misses "being absurd." Yet both his conception of himself and his dream survive everything. To its curiously actual yet unreal world, Gatsby's dream comes as "a deathless song"; in its own way it is so "absolutely real" that it changes everything it touches "into something significant, elemental, and profound." Though altogether unactual, it is its world's primary source of positive good, its primary hope of overcoming the "foul dust" and the "valley of ashes."

Before it is finally rendered "incorruptible," however, Gatsby's particular version of "the last and greatest of all human dreams" becomes a "dead dream" and leads to "grotesque" "nightmare." And it does so because, in the design through which Gatsby attempts to actualize it, it is wed to "perishable breath" and mortal mansion. In entering the round world of time-space, it falls victim to the "accidental" and ends in "holocaust." ⟨ . . . ⟩

Although it culminates in his own death, Gatsby's effort to turn dream to design and design to actuality provides the key to understanding his story. When Carraway first realizes that Gatsby's mansion is situated across the bay from Daisy's home, not by "strange coincidence", but by design, the whole of Gatsby's life begins to take form and to demand interpretation anew. "He came alive to me," Carraway says, "delivered suddenly from the womb of his purposeless splendor."

—David L. Minter, "Dream, Design, and Interpretation in *The Great Gatsby*." In *F. Scott Fitzgerald: Critical Assessments*, vol. II, ed. Henry Claridge (East Sussex: Helm Information, 1991): pp. 343–345.

[Gary Scrimgeour is the author of *A Woman of Her Times*. In this excerpt, he compares the narrators of *The Great Gatsby* and Joseph Conrad's *Heart of Darkness,* and argues that Fitzgerald's use of the first person creates several problems for the reader.]

In *Heart of Darkness* the point of the use of a first-person narrator is that what has happened to the central figure is explained by what we see happen to the narrator; and, reciprocally, the weakness evident in the central figure reveals a similar but unsuspected flaw in the character of the narrator. ⟨ . . . ⟩

A very similar relationship exists between narrator and central figure in *The Great Gatsby.* ⟨ . . . ⟩

Take, for example, Gatsby himself, a character who usually and despite Carraway's warnings wins grudging admiration from readers. Like all romantic ideals, he is what personally we would not be so foolish as to imitate but nonetheless admire for its grandeur. It is refreshing to see, without Carraway's intervening intelligence, exactly to what sort of person we are giving our sympathy. Gatsby is boor, a roughneck, a fraud, a criminal. His taste is vulgar, his behavior ostentatious, his love adolescent, his business dealings ruthless and dishonest. He is interested in people—most notably in Carraway himself—only when he wants to use them. His nice gestures stem from the fact that, as one character comments, "he doesn't want any trouble with *any*body." Like other paranoaics, he lives in a childish tissue of lies and is unaware of the existence of an independent reality in which other people have separate existences. What lifts him above ordinary viciousness is the magnitude of his ambition and the glamour of his illusion. "Can't repeat the past?" he says to Carraway. "Why of course you can. . . . " To Gatsby, to repeat the past is to suppress unwanted elements of it and to select only nice things from which to make an uncontaminated present. Grand this defiance of reality may seem; silly it nonetheless is. Indeed it is no more than "a promise that the rock of the world was founded securely on a fairy's wing," and it crumbles as soon as it encounters reality in the form of Daisy. As long as his life is controlled by his own unattained desires, Gatsby's vision remains safe; he continually recreates the present in the light of his own needs. But as soon as Daisy's independent will enters the dream, Gatsby is forced to attach himself to the real world, to lose his freedom of action, and to pay the penalty for denying the past in having that past destroy the romantic present.

Gatsby's moral error is at least as clear as Kurtz's, and yet we give him our sympathy. Sneakingly we like Gatsby, while I defy anybody to *like* Kurtz. ⟨T⟩he major reason for the difference in our attitudes to the two men is the different reactions of Carraway and Marlow to their heroes' moral weaknesses. Where Marlow ends up loathing Kurtz, Carraway specifically tells us that he is not disgusted by Gatsby but by the mysterious "foul dust that floated in the wake of his dreams." Fitzgerald provides many obscure but pretty metaphors to evoke Carraway's ambiguous attitude to Gatsby's faults, and I think he is forced into metaphor because only metaphor will conceal the fact that the story as Carraway tells it is a paean to schizophrenia. Carraway is not deceived, of course, into admiring the superficialities of Gatsby's character and behavior; he represents everything for which Carraway professes an "unaffected scorn." And yet at the same time something makes Gatsby "exempt" from Carraway's reaction to the rest of the world. Carraway tells us that Gatsby's great redeeming quality is his "heightened sensitivity to the promises of life." Whether we criticize or praise Carraway for being sufficiently young to believe that life makes promises, we should notice at once that it is the promises—not the realities—of life to which Gatsby is sensitive, and that Carraway is in fact praising that very attempt to deny the past and reality whose failure he is recounting.

—Gary Scrimgeour, "Against *The Great Gatsby.*" In *F. Scott Fitzgerald: Critical Assessments,* vol. II, ed. Henry Claridge (East Sussex, England: Helm Information, 1991): pp. 491–492.

RONALD BERMAN ON THE NEW AGENDA OF THE TWENTIES

[Ronald Berman is professor of English at the University of California, San Diego. In this excerpt, he puts *The Great*

Gatsby in its historical context and explores its attitude toward history.]

The novel begins with mention of two important events in national consciousness, the Civil War and the Great War of 1914–18. Neither holds Nick's attention for more than a moment. Hemingway was to make a career out of recollections of his war; Fitzgerald understands things differently. For him the war is a checkpoint in history, a barrier to the influence of the past. His imagination is sociological. Nick dreams neither of the past nor of the war but rather of the new agenda of the twenties—banking and credit and investment.

The postwar world is free of the past and of its institutions, but it is not free of its own false ideas. When Tom Buchanan informs Nick and the reader that "Civilization's going to pieces," he has probably never said truer words. But he is of course displaying more than he describes. He echoes a vast national debate about immigration, race, science, and art. There is something seriously wrong in America—yet it may be Tom's own class and type that is responsible. He represents a group as idle and mindless as that excoriated by Carlyle in *Past and Present*. There is something wrong with the immoral pursuit of wealth by historical figures like James J. Hill—except that inherited possession seems no better. Fitzgerald's rich boys often pose as guardians of tradition and often adduce a false relationship to public values.

The more we hear about "civilization" in the text and the more we experience its style and morality the more we, like Nick Carraway, make our own withdrawal from the historical moment. History in *The Great Gatsby* can rarely be taken at face value—perhaps it is as suspect as biography. When Tom alludes to his favorite racial or geographical or class prejudices (and when Daisy plays to them) a public dialogue is refracted. The most interesting thing about that dialogue is that many of those "advanced" people who deplore civilization in America *are considerably less attractive than Tom Buchanan*. He only echoes their discourse. What matters is not the specific character (if there is any) to his ideas about "science" or "art" but his reflection of a historical moment in which their discussion is more poisonous than his own. In the summer of 1922 there will be very little use in his appealing to profound texts or Daisy appealing to the most advanced people or Nick appealing to the values of the past—or the reader appealing to a larger and more confidence-inspiring set of standards beyond those governing the action. The allusive context of the novel is meant to disturb and disorient. It is as if Fitzgerald had Balzac in mind, and, describing a milieu in which all things are permitted, made it impossible for protagonists or readers to bring to bear morals and other norms.

As for the issue of "Civilization," that was not to be adjudicated by the defenders (and inventors) of the American past. In 1924, while Fitzgerald was thinking over the story that would become *The Great Gatsby*, the *American Mercury* (April 1924) had published a sardonic study of character acquired through consumption: It was richly attentive to certain kinds of ads that showed consumers "how to rise quickly" and "how to become" something other than they were. It noted the increased use of phrases like "wonderful," "astounding," "amazing" and "miraculously" applied to personal change and betterment. In the marketplace of ideas personal identity was itself to become a commodity.

> —Ronald Berman, *The Great Gatsby and Modern Times* (Chicago: University of Illinois Press, 1994): pp. 32–33.

WALTER BENN MICHAELS ON RACE AND RACISM

[Walter Benn Michaels is professor of English and the humanities at Johns Hopkins University, and is the author of *The Gold Standard and the Logic of Naturalism* and *Our America: Nativism, Modernism, and Pluralism*. In this excerpt he reads *The Great Gatsby* for its representation of race in the 1920s. He connects Tom Buchanan's racism to a larger cultural anxiety about what constituted a legitimate American identity.]

It is worth remembering, however, that in 1924—the year *Gatsby* was written—Klan membership was at its all-time peak, and, in fact, the Klan's style of racism finds a nonironic spokesman in *Gatsby's* Tom Buchanan explaining the argument of a book Fitzgerald calls *The Rise of the Colored Empires* by a man he calls Goddard: "The idea, [Tom says,] is that we're Nordics. . . . And we've produced all the things that go to make civilization, [but that] if we don't look out the white race will be . . . utterly submerged [by] these other races." The book Tom is speaking of was actually called *The Rising Tide of Color Against White World-Supremacy,* and its real author was Lothrop Stoddard, but Tom's paraphrase, though crude, is essentially accurate. . . . Stoddard's mission in *The Rising Tide* was to teach white men the importance of a "true race-consciousness" before it was too late, before, that is, the white race was overrun by the coloreds and before American Nordics, in particular, were drowned by the immigrant "flood" of Mediterraneans. ⟨ . . . ⟩

So, in *The Rising Tide,* non-Nordic whites have their own role to play in the rise of the colored empires, a point missed by Fitzgerald's Jordan Baker when, in response to a diatribe by Tom that begins by attacking Gatsby and ends by predicting "intermarriage between black and white," she murmurs, "We're all white here." For Tom, as for Stoddard, Gatsby (né Gatz, with his Wolfsheim "gonnegtion") isn't quite white, and Tom's identification of him as in some sense black suggests the power of the expanded notion of the alien. Gatsby's love for Daisy seems to Tom the expression of something like the impulse to miscegenation, an impulse that Nick Carraway understands as "the following of a grail. [Gatsby] knew that Daisy was extraordinary, but he didn't realize just how extraordinary a 'nice' girl could be." "Nice" here doesn't exactly mean "white," but it doesn't exactly not mean "white" either. It is a term—like "breeding"—that will serve as a kind of switching point where the Progressive novel's discourse of class will be turned into the postwar novel's discourse of race.

Comparing *The Great Gatsby* to Dreiser's *An American Tragedy,* we have already noted that when Fitzgerald's novel begins, Gatsby already has what Clyde Griffiths wants; insofar as class mobility involves transforming one's clothes, one's manners, one's friends, one's women, *The Great Gatsby* makes it almost magically easy. But Gatsby wants Daisy—the "grail"—which is to say that he wants something more or something else. The fact that he is, when they first meet, "penniless" hardly presents itself as an obstacle, partly because it can be concealed from Daisy, more importantly because it can be—and quickly is—overcome. The real problem is that he is "without a past" and to get Daisy he must get a past. Thus Jimmy Gatz's efforts to improve himself, which begin in the Franklin-like scheduling of his present intended to produce the perfected Gatsby of his future ("study electricity, etc."), must themselves be transformed into efforts to reconstruct his past: "I was brought up in America but educated at Oxford, because all my ancestors have been educated there for many years. It is a family tradition." And thus in his mind (and also, as it turns out, in hers) the key to winning Daisy back is precisely his ability to redescribe and so alter the past. ⟨ . . . ⟩

The point here is not only that the desire for a different future has been transformed into the desire for a different past but that the meaning of that past has been rendered genealogical, a matter of "ancestors."

—Walter Benn Michaels, *Our America: Nativism, Modernism, and Pluralism* (Durham: Duke University Press, 1995): pp. 23, 25–26.

Plot Summary of
Tender Is the Night

Fitzgerald wrote *Tender Is the Night* (1934) over a period of nine years, and its characters underwent constant change. Critics complain of the novel's flawed structure and its too loosely integrated themes. However, Fitzgerald's primary themes are interrelated: the loss of innocence, the effects of violence, the difficulties of love.

The novel's main conflict involves a love triangle, and this geometric shape structures the plot. Fitzgerald divides the novel into three books. The novel begins in medias res with Rosemary, who enables the reader to view the Divers from a young and bedazzled perspective. She sees their wealth and glamour as worthy aspirations. Fitzgerald uses Rosemary to develop the tragic potential of the Divers' eventual dissolution.

For some readers, Rosemary remains a minor character, and the novel's beginning thereby constitutes a "false start." However, Rosemary has an innocence appropriate to beginning: she embodies "all the immaturity of the race." Still virginal and naive, she illustrates the novel's main theme: illusions lost in coming of age. Rosemary's arrival at the shore—that threshold where sea and land meet—initiates change. This Provençal portion of the novel captures a feeling of fleeting ecstasy and youth, recalling Keats' "Ode to a Nightingale" (which provides Fitzgerald with the novel's title). Nicole's enclosed garden and the magic social congress at the Divers' dinner party appear to Rosemary as perfect pleasures. Yet the loss of innocence encroaches upon her idyll: She falls in love with Dick, and with her mother's approval, decides to pursue him, despite the fact that he is married.

Rosemary's innocence is complicated by her freedom. She illustrates the "new woman"—a cultural figure emerging from the new independence available to women through various means: the vote, increased access to education and employment, and changes in sexual mores. Economically, Rosemary is like "a boy," capable of earning her own living. The dual obstacles of marriage and age difference do not deter Rosemary from pursuing Dick. The Divers' reciprocal passion relationship piques her desire. When she overhears them plan a love tryst, she stands "breathless," while "a strong current of emotion [flows] through her." This "strong emotion" contains both emergent sexual desire for Dick, and a longing to identify with Nicole, to become like her and take her place. Likewise, Dick's age gives the affair fillip. Rosemary's innocence finds its aesthetic complement in a more experienced man, as it had in her film, *Daddy's Girl*. Watching this film, Dick recognizes "a father complex so apparent" that it makes him wince. Accustomed to playing the role of "Daddy's girl," Rosemary seeks to repeat her success with an off-screen love affair. She turns the tables on Dick by calling him "youngster" and being the pursuer rather than the pursued. Her freedom thereby makes her a threat to traditional values—like marriage—which Fitzgerald shows under pressure.

At this point, Rosemary and Dick nearly consummate their affair but other tensions interrupt the Rosemary-Dick love plot. Crisis erupts in Paris; an acquaintance of the Divers shoots her lover in the train station; Abe North mutinies against his wife's plan to send him home and goes on a drinking binge that culminates in "a dead Negro" being found in Rosemary's hotel room. Nicole's already strained nerves snap. Her mental illness recurs and precipitates a series of flashbacks (a somewhat new literary technique to the novel). Dick remembers the story's real beginning: when Nicole was even younger than Rosemary, she too was "Daddy's girl"—the victim of child sexual abuse by her father, Devereux Warren. The trauma causes schizophrenia (split personality) in the girl. Nicole's father, feeling guilty, sends Nicole to Switzerland for psychological treatment. There, Nicole encounters the young Dick Diver and begins to write to him. Her amorous feelings for Dick contribute to her cure, as she transfers her ambivalent feelings for her father onto Dick: She makes up for a disastrous incestuous affair by having a new one. Dick sees the inadvisability of their match but wants to make up for the damage Nicole's father had inflicted. Their marriage, then, represents a mutual attempt to regain Nicole's innocence, to give her the chance to marry and have a new "first love." Like Gatsby in *The Great Gatsby*, Dick thinks that Nicole can go back in time; he tells her, "Try to forget the past . . . Go back to America and be a débutante and fall in love—and be happy." Just as he does in *Gatsby*, Fitzgerald shows the delusion of such wishful thinking.

We lose our innocence as readers as well. We must ask ourselves, Was Dick's marriage to Nicole as selfless and as optimistic a gesture as he remembers? Some suspect that Dick married Nicole for her money.

Although this opinion may oversimplify the case, this plot thread gives Fitzgerald a vehicle to advance his critique of the corruptive effect of wealth. Certainly a great deal of Nicole's charm emanates from her wealth: "Nicole was the product of much ingenuity and toil. For her sake trains began their run at Chicago and traversed the round belly of the continent to California . . . as the whole system swayed and thundered onward it lent a feverish bloom to such processes of hers as wholesale buying, like the flush of a fireman's face holding his post before a spreading blaze. She illustrated very simple principles, containing in herself her own doom, but illustrated them so accurately that there was grace in the procedure . . . " Fitzgerald insists that Nicole contains "in herself her own doom" as a result of her money. Most obviously, this "doom" takes the form of her madness, which results from her father's abuse. Although wealth has its pleasures in this novel, it comes at a cost of personal integrity. Mr. Warren remains absent from the passage above and from most of the novel, but he nevertheless acts as the novel's only real villain. Reminiscent of Tom Buchanan in *The Great Gatsby*, Devereux Warren is a selfish, violent, and unscrupulous capitalist.

The novel's plot equates being rich with having a disease, and instead of curing it, Dick catches it from Nicole. Dick, like Rosemary and Nicole, loses his illusions. For all his positive attributes and his impressive background, he has his Achilles' heel: he feels incomplete and longs to be "less intact, even faintly destroyed." Fitzgerald emphasizes Dick's hubris: he wants to be all things to all people. Nicole needs him to be father, doctor, and husband. Thus he finds the role that will tire him out.

Through Dick, Fitzgerald describes a particular kind of American idealism as being tragically naive. Dick's disintegration occurs on several fronts simultaneously. For one, his financial situation strains to the breaking point. He initially refuses to be compromised by sharing Nicole's fortune but cannot refuse to share her lifestyle, and so he goes bankrupt keeping up with her. All the while, he puts this to himself in terms of maintaining his "independence." Relatedly, Dick's professional identity suffers. By marrying a mental patient, he may have permanently compromised his reputation. Instead of bringing Nicole the peace and quiet he thinks she needs, he deprives himself of it—making it nearly impossible for him to work. When Dick opens a clinic with Franz, his personal life continually intrudes: he drinks too much and he becomes too involved with the patients. When a parent accuses him of kissing an adolescent female patient, Nicole does not believe his denial. The possibility that Dick has lost his bearings and become too personal with patients seems borne out by his previous experiences, and Fitzgerald never definitively disperses the air of guilt that hangs over Dick in the second half of the novel. Dick's guilt stems ironically from a benevolent desire to help people, to be all things to them, and his plan to expand his capacity for sympathy through suffering. This tragic flaw leads him into a morass of personal compromises.

Alcohol becomes the sign of compounded personal compromises. In much of Fitzgerald's fiction, alcohol becomes the means—if not necessarily the cause—of many a violent scene, and many a ruined life. In *Tender,* alcohol initially serves a benevolent social purpose. In Provence, it seems to unite people. But the theme of innocence lost applies rigorously to alcohol: the violent events that interrupt the dinner party, like the ones that proliferate throughout the novel, repeatedly involve alcohol abuse. Dick's decline steepens as his own drinking becomes excessive. The last hurrah occurs in Rome, the fabled site of Western civilization's fall into decadence. After his father dies, Dick travels there in search of Rosemary. When he finds that they can never recapture their feeling for one another, he realizes that he has lost something profound. This realization destabilizes him. His drunken fight with the taxicab driver over a trivial amount of money shows his loss of perspective and grace. No longer able to choose and win the important battles in life, Dick becomes a victim of his own belligerence and self-importance.

How much of the blame must Nicole shoulder for Dick's ultimate failure? Or does her madness set her apart from the world of moral responsibility? Just as alcohol provides only a partial explanation for what happens to Dick in the story, so Nicole's madness may be the sign of her fallibility, if not exactly the cause of it.

Rosemary's first glimpse of Nicole on the beach presents an enigma: "Her face was hard and lovely and pitiful." That three-part description ("hard," "lovely," and "pitiful") sets up one of the novel's most profound contradictions: Nicole has all the trappings of an enviable life, yet her life is not enviable. Fitzgerald uses the term *schizophrenia,* and indeed she has a split personality: "Nicole was alternately a person to whom nothing needed to be explained and one to whom nothing could be explained."

Ultimately, the novel's lack of both a central idea and a tightly organized plot enacts the kind of confusion that lives in Nicole's mind. Some critics attribute this confusion to Fitzgerald's lack of control, and point out the mistakes he made by focusing on too many themes and characters at a time (calling attention to the beginning, for instance, as "a false start"). But this multiplicity of concerns may suggest that Fitzgerald's main theme is instability itself. Fitzgerald uses Nicole to illustrate madness in an extreme form in order to suggest, by comparison, the madness that resides in everyone to some extent. Just as Nicole has been harmed by personal tragedy, so everyone who lived through World War I, and everyone who grows up in the modern world, risks losing personal integrity.

The initial love triangle of Rosemary-Dick-Nicole is doubled in the ending: Dick-Nicole-Tommy Barban. Although the novel ends in personal tragedy for Dick, it brings Nicole a more comic result. If she had initially "transferred" her hurt and unresolved feelings for her father onto Dick, leaving him for another man represents her escape from a diseased psychological complex or spell. For Nicole, the end of the period of rapture has a positive meaning: she emerges from a state of madness into a state of clarity.

The novel seems to come full circle in other ways as well. If the novel begins with a figure of "the new woman" but leaves her to focus on Dick Diver, it then returns to the beach and to yet another figure of "the new woman." Nicole survives the plot relatively unscathed; she watches Dick's permanent disintegration from a cool distance. She makes a new start with a new husband, although she does not forget her past with Dick. And "when she [says], as she often [does], 'I loved Dick and I'll never forget him,' Tommy [answers], 'Of course not—why should you?'" ❀

List of Characters in
Tender Is the Night

Dick Diver is the novel's tragic protagonist. Having been called "Lucky Dick" as a young man, he seems to have everything at the novel's outset: intelligence, urbanity, charm, good looks, wealth, a beautiful wife and happy children. His background is impressive: son of a modest clergyman, he was educated at Yale and Johns Hopkins, was a Rhodes scholar, and studied psychiatry in Switzerland and in Vienna. Early in his medical career, he had already published a well-respected treatise. Fitzgerald identified him as "an idealist," and throughout the novel chronicles the corruption of his ideals. Paradoxically, the sources of Dick's early success become his Achilles' heel: he feels that "the price of his intactness"—his strength and integrity—is "incompleteness," and longs to be "less intact, even faintly destroyed." Thus the seeds of his destruction lie in wait within him, before he meets Nicole Warren, and long before Rosemary Hoyt. He falls in love with Nicole, perhaps hoping her illness will offer him a real challenge and give him a better chance of achieving heroism. His gradual descent into alcoholism and the obscurity of his whereabouts at the end of the novel, are both poignantly conveyed by Fitzgerald, who shared some of Dick's weaknesses.

Nicole Warren develops schizophrenia as a result of incest abuse and is hospitalized in Switzerland. There she meets psychiatrist Dick Diver and, being charmed in spite of her illness, she writes letters to him from the clinic. She is heir to a fabulous American fortune, which she shares with her older sister, Baby. Financially, she is "the product of much ingenuity and toil," being bred to spend—gracefully—the money accumulated through vast industrial exploitation of labor and material. Her shyness is punctuated by outbursts of witty, charming, and often fantastic commentary, and her perfect blonde beauty is of the kind that lasts. Her struggle with madness makes her fragile, tense, and occasionally dangerous—difficult qualities in a wife and mother. Nonetheless, she has the potential for independence, freedom, and self-realization. Certainly she is Fitzgerald's most original and interesting female character.

Rosemary Hoyt is a young movie star traveling in Europe. Rosemary falls in love with Dick Diver and decides to go "as far as she can" with the affair. The only child of a charming and ambitious widow, Rosemary has been brought up to work; "economically," she is "a boy." A combination of European boarding schools and early experience on the stage has made her thoroughly modern, deracinated, polyglot—the consummate actress. The novel shows her in the process of coming into her own: realizing her talent, her capacity to spend money, her beauty, and her sexual identity.

Baby Warren is Nicole's older sister. "Baby," as the name suggests, lives a life of arrested development; to Diver, she is "a trivial, selfish woman." She traipses around Europe in the company of other wealthy, fashionable people, acquiring a series of fiancés without ever seeming to become emotionally involved. Her anglophilia, like her love for a soldier who died in the war, indicate her persistent desire for what she cannot have. She manipulates Dick in her sister's interest. The initial heroism she exhibits when she rescues Dick from an Italian prison quickly becomes a joy of triumph over him.

Devereux Warren is Nicole's father. Despite his very brief appearances in the novel, his role in causing Nicole's initial breakdown makes him a crucial player in the story. A "strikingly handsome man," a "fine American type in every way, tall broad, well-made," he is the agent of evil in the plot. In a terminal bout with alcoholism, he attempts a death-bed reconciliation with his daughter, but then slinks, Iago-like, offstage to die alone.

Mrs. Elsie Speers is Rosemary's mother. A gracious, likable, determined woman, Mrs. Speers has widowed two husbands and raised her daughter.

Tommy Barban is Nicole's lover. The name "Barban" may suggest "barbarian" to some readers. Tommy is first and foremost a soldier for hire, without political convictions but with a strong—and wholly antiquated—honor code, bequeathed to him by his aristocratic forebears. Tommy serves as Dick's double: where Dick's good looks are fair, Tommy's are dark; where Dick is calm and nurturing, Tommy is volatile, confrontational, and hard. In Tommy, Fitzgerald caricatures a more traditional notion of masculinity in order to emphasize Diver's flawed compassion and generosity.

Abe North is a musician ruined by drink. An old friend of the Divers', Abe has already begun his decline when the novel opens. He gives the reader one of the first indications that the utopian atmosphere surrounding the Divers and their entourage has a deeper, uglier aspect. In a familiar turn of phrase, Abe North dies "in a speakeasy."

Mr. McKisco is a frustrated writer who becomes successful. In contrast to Abe North, McKisco resolves the artistic difficulties that face him at the outset of the novel, and he attains popularity. His potentially humiliating duel with Tommy Barban in Provence paradoxically gives him a new strength, and he emerges with a "vitality" that makes up for what he lacks in originality and talent.

Franz Gregorovius, a longtime professional friend of Dick Diver's, proposes the idea of opening a clinic together. Franz and his wife, **Kaethe**, share a rooted, European, quotidian sensibility that makes them less inspired and less entertaining, but more dependable than the Divers. They plod along in the paths worn smooth by tradition, having the potential neither for tragedy nor for heroism.

Collis Clay is a callow suitor for Rosemary's affections. After having taken Rosemary to a college fraternity dance at Yale, Collis Clay turns up in Europe and becomes acquainted with her new friends there.

Mary North/Contessa di Minghetti is a singer and Abe North's widow. Like Nicole and Rosemary, Mary North is a new kind of independent and ambitious woman. When Abe dies, she marries again and reappears as "the Contessa." Fitzgerald uses the occasion of a visit to her, during which the Divers manage to offend her and her new family, to show how far they have degenerated. ❁

Critical Views of
Tender Is the Night

JOHN CHAMBERLAIN ON FITZGERALD'S FALSE START

[John Chamberlain, in this contemporary review of *Tender Is the Night*, identifies the novel's beginning as "a false start."]

Mr. Fitzgerald begins well. He introduces us to a fledgling film actress, Rosemary Hoyt, a girl with the dew still on her, who is taken up by Richard and Nicole Diver during a summer stay at the Riviera. For some eighty pages or more we constantly expect Rosemary to develop, to become more and more important in the story. And then suddenly, we realize that this innocent and as yet entirely plastic girl is introduced merely as a catalytic agent. When Dick Diver, who is a psychiatrist without a practice, falls in love with Rosemary, his marriage to Nicole commences to founder. But, Rosemary, having started a chain of developments, is dismissed almost completely from the novel, and the reader pauses, at page 100, in rueful bewilderment.

In the critical terminology of Kenneth Burke, Mr. Fitzgerald has violated a "categorical expectancy." He has caused the arrows of attention to point toward Rosemary. Then, like a broken field runner reversing his field, he shifts suddenly, and those who have been chasing him fall figuratively on their noses as Mr. Fitzgerald is off on a new tack.

At this point one could almost guarantee that *Tender Is the Night* is going to be a failure. But, as a matter of fact, the novel does not really begin until Rosemary is more or less out of the way. What follows is a study of a love affair and a marriage between doctor and mental patient that is as successful a bit of writing as it must have been difficult to create in dramatic terms. Mr. Fitzgerald set himself an incredibly confused problem, but he draws the lines clearly as he works the problem out in terms of two human beings. ⟨ . . . ⟩

If, with Rosemary, he presents nothing much beyond an unformed girl, that must lie within the conception of his novel. Rosemary was evidently intended to be meaningless in herself, an unknown quantity projecting itself into a situation that merely required leverage, any leverage, to start its development toward a predictable end. The story is the story of the Divers, husband and wife, how they came together, and how they parted. As such it is a skillfully done dramatic sequence. By the time the end is reached, the false start is forgotten.

—John Chamberlain, "Books of the Times." In *F. Scott Fitzgerald: Critical Assessments,* vol. III, ed. Henry Claridge (East Sussex: Helm Information, 1991): pp. 1–3.

ALFRED KAZIN ON FITZGERALD'S VIEW OF THE RICH

[Alfred Kazin is a distinguished educator and the author of *On Native Grounds* and *F. Scott Fitzgerald: The Man and His Work.* In this essay, he evaluates Fitzgerald's condemnation of the very rich in *The Great Gatsby* and *Tender Is the Night.*]

The Great Gatsby concludes with a murder; and the true murder of Gatsby is not the crazed garage owner whose wife was Tom Buchanan's mistress, but Buchanan himself, the stupid and vicious millionaire. It was as if Fitzgerald was describing the subtle death of the will that he felt threatened by, in the form of the ultimate violence and disrespect leveled by the very rich against the truly poor. He hated the rich, for they had fascinated him too well—"they are not as we are," as he said to Hemingway. Dick Diver complains to Mary North in *Tender Is the Night:* "You're all so dull," and Mary rhapsodically flies back: "But we're all that there is! . . . All people want is to have a good time, and if you make them unhappy you cut yourselves off from nourishment." And Fitzgerald obviously believed that too, which is why he hated them even more. His notion of society, after all, was not much different from Cholly Knickerbocker's. When he read the first chapters on Michelet from Wilson's *To the Finland Station* he expressed appreciation of everything in them but the immediate content of Michelet's revolutionary interests. And when his daughter complained of some school jealousy or exclusion which humiliated her—as he could never forget how often at college he had lived on the verge of humiliation—he advised her to read the chapter on The Working Day in *Das Kapital.* "The terrible chapter . . . and see if you are ever quite the same."

Yet because the rich "were all there is," he came at last to identify them with evil. It was the revenge he played on them for having thought them life's romance. Tom Buchanan kills Gatsby; Daisy becomes as essentially vulgar and inhuman as her husband; the golf-champion whom the narrator of *The Great Gatsby* would like to love is revealed as a pathological liar; Nicole and her sister in *Tender Is the Night* fashion Dick Diver's ruin. Nicole herself rounds out the ultimate portrait of her class. She escapes madness only by parasitically marrying the psychiatrist hero, but she gives him nothing except the subtle moral bribery of her wealth. When his own decline begins she almost absentmindedly deserts him, after a gay little taste of adultery with a wealthy athlete, and the story concludes with Dick robbed of his home and children, his work and his dream of love. Standing on their beach one last hour before he leaves, Dick renders Nicole and her set a last ironic homage by making the sign of the cross over them, as Ahab said: "In the name of the devil!" The rich "are all there is," the diabolic life-force, and Dick could at least acknowledge it before he departed broken from them.

—Alfred Kazin, "Fitzgerald: An American Confession." In *F. Scott Fitzgerald: Critical Assessments*, vol. III, ed. Henry Claridge (East Sussex: Helm Information, 1991): pp. 350–351.

ROBERT STANTON ON THE INCEST MOTIF

[Robert Stanton is the author of *Introduction to Fiction.* In this essay, he explains the recurrence of incest as a motif in *Tender Is the Night*.]

The purpose of this article is to examine one of the major artistic devices used in *Tender Is the Night*. It will show that the novel contains a large number of "incest-motifs," which, properly understood, take on symbolic value and contribute to the thematic unity of the novel. The term "incest-motifs" may seem ill-chosen at first, since most of these passages allude, not to consanguineous lovers, but to a mature man's love for an immature girl. I have used the term chiefly because the first of these passages concerns Devereux Warren's incestuous relation with his fifteen-year-old daughter Nicole, so that whenever Fitzgerald later associates a mature man with an immature girl, the reader's reaction is strongly conditioned by this earlier event. Devereux's act is the most obvious, and the only literal, example of incest in the novel. It is of basic importance to the plot, since it causes Nicole's schizophrenia and thus necessitates her treatment in Dr. Dohmler's clinic, where she meets Dick Diver. Nicole's love for Dick is in part a "transference" caused by her mental disorder; the character of their marriage is dictated largely by the requirements of her condition.

In spite of the importance of Devereux's act, the use of incest as *motif* is more evident in the fact that Dick, Nicole's husband and psychiatrist, falls in love with a young actress whose most famous film is entitled *Daddy's Girl*. As this coincidence suggests, Fitzgerald deliberately gives an incestuous overtone of the relationship between Dick Diver and Rosemary Hoyt. Like Rosemary's father, Dick is of Irish descent and has been an American army doctor, a captain. At his dinner-party on the Riviera, he speaks to Rosemary "with a lightness seeming to conceal a paternal interest." He calls her "a lovely child" just before kissing her for the first time, and in the Paris hotel he says, again with a "paternal attitude," "When you smile . . . I always think I'll see a gap where you've lost some baby teeth." Dick is thirty-four, twice Rosemary's age, and to emphasize this, Fitzgerald continually stresses Rosemary's immaturity. When she first appears in 1925, her cheeks suggest "the thrilling flush of children after their cold baths in the evening"; "her body hovered delicately on the last edge of childhood—she was almost eighteen, nearly complete, but the dew was still on her." She and her mother are like "prize-winning school-children." Even Nicole pointedly refers to Rosemary as a child. ⟨ . . . ⟩

In any case, the incest-motifs may be fully accounted for by *Tender Is the Night* itself. Most of them grow logically out of Dick's relationship to Nicole. When Nicole first begins writing to Dick, she still pathologically mistrusts all men; her first letter to him speaks of his "attitude base and criminal and not even faintly what I had been taught to associate with the rôle of gentleman." Gradually Dick begins to take the place once occupied by her father, as a center of trust and security. As a psychiatrist, Dick realizes the value of this situation; he also realizes that Nicole must eventually build up her *own* world. After her psychotic attack at the Agiri fair, for example, he says, "You can help yourself most," and refuses to accept the father-role into which she tries to force him. But this sort of refusal costs him a difficult and not always successful effort of will. First, loving Nicole, "he could not watch her disintegrations without participating in them." Second, he is by nature a "spoiled priest," the father for all of his friends; he creates the moral universe in which they live. His nature and his love oppose his profession. It is therefore plausible, once his character begins to crumble, that he compensates for his long self-denial by falling in love with a girl literally young enough to be his daughter; that after the crowd has booed him for raping a five-year-old girl, he makes a mockconfession; and that when Nicole accuses him of seducing a patient's fifteen-year-old daughter, "He had a sense of guilt, as in one of those nightmares where we are accused of a crime which we recognize as something undeniably experienced, but which upon waking we realize we have not committed."

—Robert Stanton, "'Daddy's Girl': Symbol and Theme in *Tender Is the Night*." In *F. Scott Fitzgerald: Critical Assessments*, vol. III, ed. Henry Claridge (East Sussex: Helm Information, 1991): pp. 47–49.

WILLIAM DOHERTY ON KEATS' INFLUENCE

[William Doherty writes on modern literature. In this essay, he explains some of the correspondences between Keats' "Ode to a Nightingale" and Fitzgerald's *Tender Is the Night*.]

It is true that the title *Tender Is the Night* was chosen late in the extended course of the book's writing; but it seems clear that Fitzgerald was conscious of the "Ode" not merely in the last stages of composition. The title is appropriate, though no one has said why. Yet, a moment's reflection will show that there is a good deal of Keatsian suggestiveness in *Tender Is the Night* in both decor and atmosphere—the Provençal summers of sunburnt mirth, the night perfumed and promising, the dark gardens of an illusory world. ⟨ . . . ⟩

The brief transport from the world which the "Ode" details, the emotional adventure of climax and decline is suggested in this and in a number of other scenes in *Tender Is the Night*. Indeed, the pattern describes the very rhythm of the novel. The party at the Villa Diana, as Malcolm Cowly suggests, appears to be the high point in the story. The scene marks a change of mood; thereafter, the light romantic atmosphere is dispelled. We see there the Divers at their point of greatest charm—a "vision of ease and grace," commanding all the delicacies of existence. It is a high point for another reason. It is in this scene that the principals of the story make an escape from the prosaic and temporal world. In the rarefied atmosphere of the party a moment is caught in which a delicate triumph over time is achieved.

The party is given out of doors in the garden, Nicole's garden. To Rosemary the setting seems to be the center of the world: "On such a stage some memorable thing was sure to happen." The guests arrive under a spell, bringing with them the excitement of the night. ⟨ . . . ⟩

This garden, the fireflies riding on the dark air, the summer evening, the wine-colored lanterns hung in the trees—the Romantic decor is there, and the Keatsian atmosphere: "the diffused magic of the hot sweet South . . . the soft-pawed night and the ghostly wash of the Mediterranean far below." There is no need to insist that these images have their antecedents in the "Ode"—in its "murmurous haunt of flies on summer eves, " or its "warm south," its "tender night," its charmed magic casements opening on perilous seas"; for the clearest parallel to the poem lies in the brief achievement of the precious atmosphere, achieved through the familiar Romantic formula of escape at the moment of emotional pitch—here ironically, a moment of sexual ecstasy, but suggesting inevitably the dynamics of the sexual event. The imagery itself reiterates the pattern: the fragile loveliness of Nicole's garden increases "until, as if the scherzo of color could reach no further intensity, it broke off suddenly in midair, and moist steps went down to a level five feet below."

—William Doherty, "*Tender Is the Night* and 'Ode to a Nightingale.'" In *Modern Critical Views: F. Scott Fitzgerald,* ed. Harold Bloom (New York: Chelsea House, 1985): pp. 182–185.

[Arthur Mizener was professor of English at Cornell University. In addition to numerous other publications he authored *The Far Side of Paradise*, a literary biography of F. Scott Fitzgerald. In this essay, he compares Fitzgerald's representation of the appeal of the Divers and the rich as opposed to the pretending McKisco group.]

⟨I⟩n the end ⟨Fitzgerald⟩ came to feel that the unimaginative brutality and organized chaos of the life of the rich always defeated men like Dick Diver. In Dick's best moment, *Tender Is the Night* shows us how beautiful the realized ideal life is; but in the end it shows us that people with the sensitivity and imagination to conceive that life cannot survive among the rich.

Tender Is the Night begins with the arrival of a young movie star named Rosemary Hoyt at Cap d'Antibes on the Riviera. When Rosemary goes down to the beach she finds herself between two groups of expatriates. The first is an incoherent mixture. There is "Mama" Abrams, "one of those elderly 'good sports' preserved by an imperviousness to experience and a good digestion into another generation." There is a writer named Albert McKisco who, according to his wife, Violet, is at work on a novel "on the idea of Ulysses. Only instead of taking twenty-four hours [he] takes a hundred years. He takes a decayed old French aristocrat and puts him in contrast with the mechanical age. . . . " There is a waspishly witty young man named Royal Dumphry and his companion, Luis Campion, who keeps admonishing Mr. Dumphry not to "be too ghastly for words." The other group consists of Dick Diver and his wife, Nicole, their friends Abe and Mary North, and a young Frenchman named Tommy Barban.

Rosemary is instinctively attracted to the second group but she is quickly picked up by the first group, who cannot wait to tell her they recognize her from her film. It is not a very happy group. For one thing, it is clearly jealous of the second group. "If you want to enjoy yourself here," Mrs. McKisco says, "the thing is to get to know some real French families. What do these people get out of it? They just stick around with each other in little cliques. Of course we had letters of introduction and met all the best French artists and writers in Paris." For another thing, Mr. McKisco is being difficult, as if, in spite of his extensive collection of secondhand attitudes from the best reviews, he does not quite know who he is or where he is going. When his wife makes a harmless joke, he bursts out irritably, "For God's sake, Violet, drop the subject! Get a new joke, for God's sake!" and when she leans over to Mrs. Abrams and says apologetically, "He's nervous," Mr. Mc-Kisco barks, "I'm not nervous. It just happens I'm not nervous at all."

It is the poverty of ideas and the mediocrity of imagination in these people, the shapelessness of their natures, that depresses and discomforts Rosemary and makes her dislike them. It is her glimpses of the opposite qualities in the second group that attracts her. What Rosemary sees in Dick Diver is his consideration, his grace, his sensitivity to others, and—behind them all—his intense vitality. No wonder she falls in love with him.

—Arthur Mizener, "*Tender Is the Night.*" In *Modern Critical Views: F. Scott Fitzgerald,* ed. Harold Bloom (New York: Chelsea House, 1985): pp. 102–103.

ALAN TRACHTENBERG ON SEPARATE POINTS OF VIEW

[Alan Trachtenberg is professor of American Studies and English at Yale University and is the author of *The Incorporation of America.* In this essay, he discusses the historical connotations of both Nicole's recovery and her relationship to Tommy Barban.]

Like Rosemary's and Dick's in the earlier books, Nicole's point of view in Book Three is not the sole perspective. The reader has been creating what might be called a perspective of the story as a whole, a perspective which contains each separate point of view as it does each separate episode. The way Nicole sees the world has a social history and a social content developed within the process of the narrative. As we have seen in the shifting patterns of imagery, a basic feature of that process is the instability of appearances. Apparently dominant facts and impressions contain opposite possibilities, as the book's present contains a thoroughly unlikely future. Thus the pathos of a sick Nicole, a "waif of disaster," had obscured the potentiality of a healthy Nicole. In Book One, in an intrusive but remarkable passage, we learn to anticipate the restoration of Nicole's social history: she was, we learn, "the product of much ingenuity and toil," an expression, even in her trauma, of an entire social system, for whose sake "trains began their run at Chicago . . . chicle factories fumed . . . men mixed toothpaste in vats . . . girls canned tomtoes . . . half-breed Indians toiled on Brazilian coffee plantations. . . . " Thus "she illustrates very simple principles, containing in herself her own doom, but illustrated them so accurately that there was grace in the procedure." Grace and doom coexist in her as historical inheritances, and as we observe her throughout the novel we are preparing to recognize what will happen in the end: the fulfillment of her grace, the accuracy of her restored character as an illustration of the selfish morality of her social class, is identical with her doom. "'I'm well again,'" she tells Tommy Barban. "'And being well perhaps I've gone back to my true self—I suppose my grandfather was a crook and I'm a crook by heritage.'" (Earlier we had learned that her rich grandfather had begun his career as a horse thief.) Nicole's surrender to Tommy is given an even wider range of historical connotation in the following passage: "Moment by moment all that Dick taught her fell away and she was ever nearer to what she had been in the beginning, prototype of that obscure yielding up of swords that was going on in the world about her. Tangled with love in the moonlight she welcomed the anarchy of her lover."

Nicole's fulfillment, which is a journey back to her true nature, occurs in time, "moment by moment." It is historical in the personal sense of her individual development in the novel, and also in a larger sense that the novel forces upon us: the transfer of her allegiance, her money, and the power it represents, to a new force typified by a counterrevolutionary mercenary turned stockbroker. Nicole's yielding to Barban becomes an emblem of the yielding of order to disorder, as the crumbling actions of Book Three make clear. The outlaw lovers come together as each other's present opportunity for personal and social survival. In the final scene on the Riviera, Nicole "got to her knees" in a momentary and automatic response to Dick's "papal cross" over the beach that was once his "bright tan prayer mug"; when Tommy pulls "her firmly down," he exercises the discipline she requires to complete her liberation from Dick, and thus certifies the social character of her new self.

—Alan Trachtenberg, "The Journey Back: Myth and History in *Tender is the Night*." In *F. Scott Fitzgerald: Critical Assessments,* vol. III, ed. Henry Claridge (East Sussex: Helm Information, 1991): pp. 138–139.

JAMES GINDIN ON DIVER'S FAILURE

[James Gindin is the author of *British Fiction in the 1930's: The Dispiriting Decade,* and has taught English at the University of Michigan. In this essay, he reads Dick Diver as a rebellious son in search of a paternal model.]

Dick may believe in two worlds, the moral one of the old America and the new one of his women, but he cannot live in both. And as he fails, his own morality, his own center, begins to dissolve. He works less and less, becomes more dependent on Nicole's money, and is increasingly drunken, careless, and inconsiderate. When Rosemary Hoyt, who had once idolized him, tells him that he still seems the man he was, he replies, "The manner remains intact for some time after the morale cracks"—almost as if he is Dorian Gray with a deeply imbedded sense of sin just under an easy façade. Dick's "manner" eventually cracks, too, for he becomes violent and petulant, picks fights, indulges in self-pity, and is pointlessly vulgar in talking with Nicole. All these are symptoms of an advanced stage of dissolution: for Fitzgerald, not behaving well, not observing superficial amenities and conventions, always indicates the hero's irreversible defeat.

The doom is not as elemental and universal as that of *The Great Gatsby,* for *Tender Is the Night* is a more complicated novel. For example, the father figures proliferate, suggesting a more equivocal morality than that of *The Great Gatsby.* Dick's real father is an American clergyman who had taught Dick all he knew of "manners" and "matters of behavior," a man halfway between Nick Carraway's wise and sophisticated father and Gatsby's humble simpleton. Though honest and direct, he lacks the intellect, the range, and the insight to be transportable to the new and more complicated world of postwar Europe. Despite the distance in space and time between Dick and his father, Dick often "referred judgments to what his father would probably have thought or done." Yet he recognizes that, in choosing Europe, he has abandoned his father. He temporarily returns to America to attend his father's funeral: "These dead, he knew them all, their weather-beaten faces with blue flashing eyes, the spare violent bodies, the souls made of new earth in the forest-heavy darkness of the seventeenth century. 'Good-by, my father—good-by, all my fathers.'" Dick attaches himself to a surrogate father, Dr. Dohmler, the psychiatrist in charge of the clinic where Dick initially works. Dr. Dohmler is fiercely moral, an instructor, a guide, and Dick is strongly influenced by his precepts and judgments. Yet in marrying Nicole, in confusing the separate relationships between husband and wife and between doctor and patient, Dick disobeys one of Dr. Dohmler's strongest injunctions. The real father is not necessarily preferable to the surrogate, for either might have served to transmit his morality to Dick. But Dick abandons one and disobeys the other; left alone, he cannot sustain himself. The father also has responsibilities toward his child: Nicole's father, in forcing incest upon her, actually converts his daughter into his mistress and so violates the relationship between father and child in the most disastrous way possible.

—James Gindin, "Gods and Fathers in F. Scott Fitzgerald's Novels." In *Modern Critical Views: F. Scott Fitzgerald*, ed. Harold Bloom (New York: Chelsea House, 1985): pp. 119–120.

MARY E. BURTON ON FREUDIAN THEORY

[Mary E. Burton has taught at the University of California and written on Wordsworth's *Prelude*. In this essay, she explains the psychiatric and psychoanalytic concepts of transference and counter-transference and their place in the novel.]

In simple words, Dick has studied Jung, but basically he is a Freudian. As such he must be cognizant of the original neurosis Freud had treated—female hysteria caused by either real or fantasied rape of the patients by their fathers—and also of two of Freud's chief theoretical discoveries: those of transference and counter-transference. Ripe with

66

this knowledge he comes back to Dr. Gregorovious' clinic, meets, falls in love with, and marries the adorably pretty neurotic Nicole, victim of just such a father-seduction, and through his love for her is, inevitably, destroyed. The heart of the matter is, then, why does Lucky Dick, analytic Dick, forewarned and forearmed Dick, make this disastrous choice of mate, and how and why is the counter-transference which destroys him effected?

In Freudian theory treatment of neurosis, transference as a part of therapy is essential and necessary. The psychiatrist allows and encourages the patient to play out or talk out before him the problems, dreams, anxieties most distressing to him, while himself remaining a neutral non-reacting "blank face," permitting all, anonymous and discreet. Gradually the patient begins to focus on the persons or person (usually a parent) who is most troublesome to him and begins to behave to the doctor as if the doctor were that parent. But the doctor refuses to "play back," insisting that the patient work through and analyse his own problems, correcting the patient when he goes astray from the central theme, guiding him by example, support and encouragement to rid himself of the neurosis and begin to lead a life more consistent with reality. If transference is completed, the cure is hopeful.

Counter-transference, on the other hand, is a very dangerous situation, both for doctor and patient. Here the psychiatrist, instead of being the uninvolved blank face begins to involve himself with the patient's neurotic situation: for example, a young girl patient whose problem is her hidden desire for her father plays this role out in front of the psychiatrist who, through weaknesses of his own, actually starts behaving like the desired forbidden parent. (The incidence of psychiatrists who fall in love with their patients is not statistically recorded, but is fairly well known to anyone who has frequented therapeutic circles.) ⟨ . . . ⟩

But why the love-marriage? ⟨ . . . ⟩

The basic reason for Dick's fascination with Nicole, finally his absorption into her very being ⟨ . . . ⟩ is exposed in a highly significant early meditation of Dick's. Back in his Vienna days Dick muses to himself, "'And Lucky Dick can't be one of these clever men' [he has been doubting the quality of his own mind *vis-a-vis* Freud, Adler, Jung]; 'he must be less intact, even faintly destroyed. If life won't do it for him it's not a substitute to get a disease, or a broken heart, or an inferiority complex, though it'd be nice to build out some broken side till it was better than the original structure.'" The metaphor of the broken side has an appalling reality. Dick is at least preconsciously aware that he has already been "broken" by the American dream, that his "broken side" (Adam's rib) is that side of him from which the American Aphrodite has been born—she who is, henceforth, his chosen mate and destiny. ⟨ . . . ⟩ He will not renounce the dream or fully recognize the neurosis which pervades him; he will not bring himself to compromise with reality—for compromise seems to every romantic a reduction. Instead, he will dare to "fly with the light-winged Dryad," "mid-May's eldest child" of Keats's poem, through "charm'd magic casements, opening on the foam"; he will take his dream to heart and create of it a work of art. Pygmalion-like, he will bring Nicole to life, and in doing so, transcend the American neurosis into a beatific vision of the romantic dream.

—Mary E. Burton, "The Counter-Transference of Dr. Diver." In *Modern Critical Views: F. Scott Fitzgerald,* ed. Harold Bloom (New York: Chelsea House, 1985): pp. 130–133.

Edwin T. Arnold on Movies as Metaphor

[Edwin T. Arnold has written books on Robert Aldrich, Erskine Caldwell, Cormac McCarthy, and William Faulkner. In this excerpt, he explores the metaphoric importance of the movies to various characters in *Tender Is the Night.*]

⟨I⟩n the first part of *Tender,* Dick Diver seems to be very much in control of not only his and Nicole's lives, but also the lives of everyone else who enters his sphere of influence. He is described as a director in connection with his parties. ⟨ . . . ⟩

Dick keeps everything in control, and this is one of the main things that attracts the actress, Rosemary Hoyt, to him. She is, at this stage of her life, in need of a director, a position previously held by her mother, for Rosemary's life is largely a matter of acting and posing. When she convinces herself that she loves Dick and arranges to throw herself at him, she is "astonished at herself—she had never imagined she could talk like that. She was calling on things she had read, seen, dreamed through a decade of convent hours. Suddenly she knew too that it was one of her greatest roles and she flung herself into it more passionately." Still, although Rosemary indulges herself in some self-deluding romanticizing, she is far beyond being fooled by it; she is "In the movies but not at all At them." ⟨ . . . ⟩

Dick has a certain snobbery concerning actors and acting. Yet his adamant refusal to take a screen test which Rosemary has arranged for him reveals a basic weakness of his character:

> "I don't want a test," said Dick firmly. . . . "The pictures make a fine career for a woman—but my God, they can't photograph me. . . . The strongest guard is placed at the gateway to nothing," he said. "Maybe because the condition of emptiness is too shameful to be divulged." ⟨ . . . ⟩

He fears having to look at himself, having to recognize the actor in him, and having to acknowledge the "condition of emptiness" which the mask of the actor disguises. ⟨ . . . ⟩

What Fitzgerald quite clearly marks as a "turning point" in Dick's life occurs on the day he goes to the movie studio to meet Rosemary, in effect, to enter into her world of illusion: "He knew that what he was now doing . . . was out of line with everything that had preceded it—even out of line with what effect he might hope to produce upon Rosemary. Rosemary saw him always as a model of correctness—his presence walking around this block was an intrusion." ⟨ . . . ⟩

⟨I⟩t is at this point that the motif of the actor rather than the director takes over in Fitzgerald's description of Dick. As he stands outside the studio, which is located in a "melancholy neighborhood," surrounded by signs of "Life and death," he begins to realize that his "necessity of behaving as he did was a projection of some submerged reality: he was compelled to walk there, or stand there. . . . Dick was paying some tribute to things unforgotten, unshriven, unexpurgated."

Rosemary seems immediately to recognize the reversal of her and Dick's roles, for when they are finally alone together in her room, Rosemary "stood up and leaned down and said her most sincere thing to him:

'Oh, we're such *actors*—you and I.'"

And when they leave, "Dick clung to the situation; Rosemary was first to return to reality.

'I must go, youngster,' she said."

As her calling him "youngster" indicates, Rosemary has gained, and knows that she has gained, the upper hand in their relationship.

Dick's disintegration follows.

—Edwin T. Arnold, "The Motion Picture as Metaphor in the Works of F. Scott Fitzgerald." In *Fitzgerald/Hemingway Annual*, ed. Margaret M. Duggan and Richard Layman (Detroit: Gale Research Co., 1977): pp. 53–55.

BRIAN WAY ON ACTS OF VIOLENCE

[Brian Way is the author of *F. Scott Fitzgerald and the Art of Social Fiction* (1980). In this excerpt, he explores Fitzgerald's emphasis on violence in the novel.]

What disturbs Fitzgerald most in expatriate life however—as in the Jazz Age generally—is its tendency to break out in arbitrary acts of violence or swift personal catastrophes. In *Tender Is the Night*, the quality of such events is represented most clearly by the murder of the negro Peterson. A fortuitous chain of circumstances, which begins when Abe North is involved in a drunken dispute in a Montmartre bar, ends with the appearance of Peterson's corpse on Rosemary's bed. In its dramatic and psychological effect, the episode is shocking and unexpected, but in a more fundamental sense, it is typical—just as Abe's own death is appalling and yet predictable.

From the very beginning, Fitzgerald believed that the American adventure of the 1920s, through its lack of restraint and its absence of style, was bound to end in disaster. As early as 1920, in his short story 'May Day', Fitzgerald had tried to use the suicide of Gordon Sterrett as a way of expressing his sense of this tendency. One of the most urgent problems he faced as a historian of manners was that of finding the right image of disaster. It is this difficulty—far more than his drinking, Zelda's illness, or the need to write magazine stories for money—which explains why it took him nine years to write *Tender Is the Night*. . . . Zelda's mental breakdown, and Fitzgerald's own complex sense of failure, finally gave him sufficiently precise knowledge of the mechanisms of disaster. This is not to say that *Tender Is the Night* is an autobiographical novel, but merely to point out that a novelist can only use those parts of his observation and experience which are within the scope of his artistic talents. There was nothing in Fitzgerald's fictional methods that enabled him to deal with climactic acts of violence, but he was superbly fitted to evoke subtle psychological states and finally shaded social situations. In the final version of the novel, he discovered how to make violence part of an atmosphere, and personal catastrophe a matter of slow disintegration and hidden suffering.

—Brian Way, *F. Scott Fitzgerald and the Art of Social Fiction* (London: Edward Arnold Ltd., 1980): pp. 141–142.

RONALD J. GERVAIS ON SOCIALISM AND CAPITALISM

[Ronald J. Gervais has taught at San Diego State University and is the author of *Mark Twain and the Fall into Moral Sense*. In this essay, he explores the conflicting attitudes toward socialism and capitalism in *Tender Is the Night*.]

⟨Elsewhere, Fitzgerald⟩ seems to suggest a fatal attraction that the material beauties of capitalism have for even the most idealistic and ascetic of socialists. ⟨ . . . ⟩

Tender Is the Night (1934) shows the same pattern. But Dick Diver's debate is more within himself. His idealism is bought out by the sick and dying yet still beautiful and captivating capitalist class that he had hoped to save. The "General Plan" of 1932 for the novel calls Dick "in fact a communist—liberal—idealist, a moralist in revolt." The tension between such commitments and Diver's compulsive tenderness for the psychoses of the leisure class suggests the conflicts that must have moved Fitzgerald while writing this novel.

Dick Diver's "communist" sympathies express themselves practically only in a suggestion, left out of the final version, that he would send his son to the Soviet Union to educate him, "thus having accomplished both his burgeoisie [*sic*] sentimental ideals in the case of his wife and his ideals in the case of his son." Another vestige of the plan may also be seen in the fierce anti-communism of Dick's rival for Nicole, Tommy Barban. Tommy has fought the Soviets under Kor-niloff, the White Russian general, and leaves two young Red Guards dead at the border in helping an old Tsarist aristocrat to escape. But Fitzgerald's mixed intentions are indicated by his making the fatuous *arriviste* Albert McKisco the only avowed socialist in the novel. "Why do you want to fight the Soviets?" McKisco argues with Tommy Barban before their duel. "The greatest experiment ever made by humanity?" ⟨ . . . ⟩

⟨Eventually⟩, his intention to have Dick Diver be a communist was dropped, he explained in 1935, in order to make him "a living romantic idealist," "an individual," rather than "a type." Dick is finally even described in the novel as being "poor material for a socialist," because his personal ambition to do rare work cuts him off from sympathy with the masses—"God, am I like the rest after all?"

Fitzgerald's love for the romantic possibilities of individualism, against any concept of collectivism, puts him ambivalently on the side of the most individualistic of all socio-economic systems, even when he sees that its freedom has become ruinous. His description of Nicole's shopping trip in *Tender Is the Night* is both an indictment of the moneyed aristocracy and a wonder-song to the glittering life-style open to them. ⟨ . . . ⟩ Despite its impending doom, the way of life open to the rich is infinitely charming. Its "feverish bloom" and "grace" are insidiously beguiling even to Dick Diver, whose ascetic

ideology of the old Protestant work ethic never quite finds an exten-
sion in outright radicalism against the spending and gratification of
consumer capitalism.

—Ronald J. Gervais, "The Socialist and the Silk Stockings: Fitzgerald's
Double Allegiance," In *Modern Critical Views: F. Scott Fitzgerald*, ed.
Harold Bloom (New York: Chelsea House, 1985): pp. 172–174.

JUDITH FETTERLY ON SEXUAL POLITICS

[Judith Fetterly is professor at the State University of New
York, Albany. She is the author of *The Resisting Reader* and
American Women Regionalists, 1850–1910. In this essay, she
explores the feminine side of Dick Diver's character.]

Rosemary needs only one morning on the beach to discover that Dick
Diver has created a world, to realize that those who are not part of it
wish they were, and to long to become part of it herself.

Dick's capacity for creating such worlds is not limited to the
setting of the beach. Dick—not Nicole—gives dinner parties.
Dick orchestrates his dinner party from beginning to end, from
the moment of invitation to the moment of departure, and the
special feeling that the guests take away with them from the occasion is *his* gift. Dick's party recalls a similar event in Virginia
Woolf's *To The Lighthouse*. The force of the comparison for our
purposes resides, of course, in the degree to which it identifies
Dick Diver as engaging in a quintessentially feminine activity. For
Woolf's text is culturally accurate—women do give dinner parties; the daily round of meals and the sense of community and so-
ciability associated with them are a part of women's "job,"
women's work. Woolf also recognizes that the threats to the community created through the art of female nurturance come from
the ugly intrusion of various male egos all clamoring to be fed. In
Tender Is the Night, the reversal of roles is completed when Nicole
emerges as the threat to the sense of community created by Dick.
Her breakdown constitutes the ugly intrusion into his world,

converting the delicate sense of communion which is his gift into the vulgarity of the consequent duel.

If Dick is engaged in feminine activity, he has the character traits which go with it—tact, delicacy of feeling, consideration for and sensitivity to others. ⟨ . . . ⟩ Men talk and women listen, but Dick is not like most men. ⟨ . . . ⟩

Women respond to Dick as if he were a woman, or, perhaps more accurately, women treat Dick the way men usually treat women. Women appropriate Dick for his services and value him for his usefulness to them. His ability to handle the mess engendered by Abe North's unexpected, unannounced and drunken return to Paris saves Rosemary's reputation. Similarly, his final service, before dismissal, is undertaken to preserve the reputation of Mary North. And, of course, after his marriage his whole life is dedicated to the service of Nicole. Baby Warren lays it on the line with her talk about buying Nicole a doctor and with her casual evaluation of Dick's suitability for temporary service. More subtly, Mrs. Speers evaluates Dick's usefulness, giving Rosemary the go-ahead only after she has decided that Dick is the "real thing," capable of adding significantly to Rosemary's education and development, and not a "spurious substitute" who might damage her. Indeed, Mrs. Speers gladly places Rosemary in and on Dick's hands, anticipating the rest that will ensue for herself should her daughter's "exigent idealism . . . focus on something" other than her mother. Thus, in his affair with Rosemary, Dick serves both mother and daughter. Of reciprocal concern for himself, there is none: "He saw that no provisions had been made for him . . . in Mrs. Speers' plans."

But Rosemary and Nicole fall in love with Dick at first sight; indeed, they fall in love with Dick in precisely the same way that Jay Gatsby falls in love with Daisy Buchanan: the first "nice" girl is simply transposed to the first "nice" man. The role reversal inherent in this parallelism receives its finishing touch from the fact that both Rosemary and Nicole remain curiously detached from the process of "falling in love" and essentially invulnerable to it. Thus Rosemary's mother launches her on her affair with Dick with the blessing, "You were brought up to work—not especially to marry. . . . Wound yourself or him—whatever happens it can't spoil you because economically you're a boy, not a girl." And at the end of the novel, it is Dick who is destroyed by love, not Nicole.

—Judith Fetterly, "Who Killed Dick Diver?: The Sexual Politics of *Tender Is the Night.*" In *F. Scott Fitzgerald: Critical Assessments,* vol. III, ed. Henry Claridge (East Sussex: Helm Information, 1991): pp. 211–212.

GENE PHILLIPS ON THE OUTCOME FOR DIVER

[The Reverend Gene D. Phillips is professor of English at Loyola University in Chicago. In this excerpt, he evaluates Dick's relationship to the Warrens and his status as a hero, martyr, and "spoiled priest."]

The Warrens' self-centered creed is epitomized in Nicole's sister, whose nickname, "Baby," aptly describes her as a selfish child at heart. Baby Warren encourages Nicole to marry Dick because she feels that if Nicole's therapist is also her husband, this will insure that he will devote himself almost exclusively to Nicole, who subconsciously sees Dick as a kind of substitute father. As Dick becomes more and more enmeshed in the Warren family's personal problems, which involve nothing less than incest and insanity, he begins to see himself as "the last hope of a decaying clan." But gradually he comes to realize that, to his shame, he has sold his career as a psychiatrist to the Warrens on the installment plan. In effect Dick has permitted himself to be "swallowed up like a gigolo," and has somehow allowed his professional abilities "to be locked up in the Warren safety-deposit vaults." ⟨ . . . ⟩

⟨W⟩hen Dick has depleted the last of his store of psychic reserves in helping his wife regain her sanity and is therefore of no further use to her or the family, Nicole, at Baby's urging, callously leaves him for the crass Philistine Tommy Barban (short for barbarian?). After Nicole walks out on him, Dick finds that he has sunk into a state of complete emotional exhaustion, and no longer wants anything more out of life than to fade "at last into the tender night, where he hopes nothing will ever be required of him again." The stag at eve has had his fill.

Since Dick had allowed himself to be bought by the Warrens, Fitzgerald fittingly describes Dick's psychological condition at the end of the novel in financial terms: emotional bankruptcy. Fitzgerald's point is that Dick invested all of his emotional capital in Nicole, both as her husband and her doctor; and when he had spent it all on her and had nothing left to give, she and the rest of the family abandoned him. But the novelist does not mean to imply that Dick is a martyr or a saint. In the final outline of the novel's action, dated 1932, Fitzgerald goes on to call Dick a "spoiled priest" who has renounced his vocation as a healer of the spirit for an empty life of "drink and dissipation." By novel's end, then, one wonders if Dick Diver, whose once promising career has finally taken a nose dive, will ever be able to pull himself out of the lower depths; but Fitzgerald offers no clear forecast.

Still, his father's life of pastoral service as a clergyman, which Dick reflects upon more than once in the course of the novel, remains an undiminished source of inspiration for Dick, who had once consecrated himself to be a physician of the soul. In fact, it is possibly out of reverence for his father's memory that Dick makes a symbolic gesture just as he is about to depart the Riviera for good. He turns toward the shore one last time, and from the terrace on which he stands, he makes the Sign of the Cross over his loved ones down on the beach whom he is leaving behind, in much the same manner that his father would have bestowed his blessing on his flock. Despite Dick's fall from grace, then, one infers that perhaps his father will continue to be an abiding reminder of the sort of dedicated person he himself once was, and hopefully can be again.

—Gene D. Phillips, *Fiction, Film, and F. Scott Fitzgerald* (Chicago: Loyola University Press, 1986): pp. 130–131.

SARAH FRYER ON WOMEN'S POWERLESSNESS

[In this excerpt, Sarah Beebe Fryer praises Fitzgerald's insightful and realistic portrayal of Nicole as a victim of incest, and goes on to explore that victimization as a metaphoric representation of larger social ills faced by women.]

In *Tender Is the Night,* more than in any of his other novels, Fitzgerald captures the nature of the impact conventional male chauvinism could have on a woman of his era. While the principal female character in all of his other novels struggle with comparatively subtle forms of patriarchal oppression, Nicole Warren Diver is victimized by overt sexual exploitation perpetuated both by her father and by her psychiatrist-husband. According to contemporary theories, the dynamics of her illness and her interactions with men in general are startlingly appropriate for an incest victim. Moreover, her vulnerability to "rape" by her father and subsequent exploitation by her father surrogate, a psychiatrist with whom she has a transference, can be viewed symbolically as a reflection of the New Woman's tenuous social position in the face of patriarchal traditions. It is therefore important to examine Nicole's confusion about her experiences and roles in considerable detail. ⟨ . . . ⟩

Regardless of how Fitzgerald obtained the incest material he used in his creation of Nicole, however, his evident grasp of the vulnerabilities of an incest victim is irrefutable. His literary portrait of Nicole—her sometimes irrational behavior; her unwarranted faith in Dick; her poor self-esteem; her dependency; her longings for health, work and respect—reads like a case study of a hysteric (not a schizophrenic) whose illness was precipitated by incest. Nicole's "madness," which is often exaggerated and seen as the root of all Dick's problems, can be explained very readily with the help of late twentieth-century psychological research on incest victims and women who become sexually involved with their therapists.

In fact, as a result of Fitzgerald's perhaps intuitive understanding of the ramifications of incest, Nicole's tragedy is somewhat easier to comprehend—in a psychological and sociological context—than Dick's, though the novel is generally treated as Dick Diver's story. ⟨ . . . ⟩

Nicole's experience of incest is important to the novel in that it shapes her character, evokes her illness, and makes her profoundly vulnerable to Dick's objectification of her. She is twice victimized—first by incest and then by psychiatric malpractice; both manifestations of exploitation stem directly from patriarchal traditions that accord women second-class citizenship. Perhaps unbeknownst to Fitzgerald, the incest in *Tender Is the Night* serves metaphorically as a reminder of women's powerlessness in traditional patriarchal societies. The family where a father "rapes" a daughter, like the "therapeutic" relationship that allows men to define women's reality, is a microcosm of a larger society that condones and perpetuates myriad means of exploiting and subjugating women. Nicole's relentless efforts to rise above her dual victimization are the efforts of a New Woman envisioning equality an autonomy.

—Sarah Beebe Fryer, "Fitzgerald's New Women," *Studies in Modern Literature* 86, ed. A. Walton Litz and Jackson R. Bryer (Ann Arbor, MI: UMI Research Press, 1988): pp. 71–72, 74.

JOHN WILLIAM CROWLEY ON THE DRUNKARD'S HOLIDAY

[John William Crowley is the author of *The White Logic: Alcoholism and Gender in American Modernist Fiction* (1994). In this extract Crowley explores the theme of alcoholism in Fitzgerald's life and fiction.]

The most significant of Fitzgerald's fictions about drinking is *Tender Is the Night* (1934), the locus classicus of American drunk narratives, in which a drunkard's tragic downfall is played out against a backdrop of Spenglerian cultural decline. Dick Diver's alcoholism reflected that of his author, whose own life was falling apart during the nine years he struggled to finish the novel, which at one point in its evolution was titled "The Drunkard's Holiday." "It is apparent," as Tom Dardis says, "that Fitzgerald, by using alcohol as both cause *and* effect in the creation of Diver's malaise, was drawing a parallel between his fictional couple and Zelda and himself." Although he does not emphasize Diver's drinking until late in the novel, he nevertheless "permits us to observe that nearly all of Dick's troubles—professional and marital—have alcohol behind them."

Against such assertions Diver might have argued, as Fitzgerald himself once testily remarked, "The assumption that all my troubles are due to drink is a little too easy." ⟨ . . . ⟩

Although it *would* be reductive to use alcoholism either as a single-cause explanation for Fitzgerald's life or as a skeleton key to his work, drinking was undoubtedly the efficient cause of his decline, and it had complex literary consequences.

It is easy, for example, to read the alcohol-related fiction too literally, as if it were uncomplicated by Fitzgerald's need to excuse his drinking at the same time as he pretended to face up to it. ⟨ . . . ⟩

Throughout Fitzgerald's life and work, as Marty Roth observes, a curious paradox about drinking persists: it is everywhere and yet nowhere, manifest and yet invisible. In *The Great Gatsby,* for instance, there is "a great deal of drinking and much drunken behavior," but the voluminous criticism on the novel is virtually silent about these matters. This critical silence strikes Roth as "equivalent to both the social and medical invisibility of alcoholism." Drinking "is there but nobody sees it, or, if it is there to be seen, it is not connected to anything else." Thus in the first scene of *The Great Gatsby,* "the drinks are not seen attached to anyone: the four cocktails are 'just in from the pantry' as if on their own. . . . And earlier Nick had written that '[a] tray of cocktails floated at us through the twilight.'" ⟨ . . . ⟩

Once it is recognized that the inner logic of Diver's character derives from his alcoholism, interpretative difficulties seem to melt away. With rare exceptions, however, any such recognition has eluded the critics. How can it be that resourceful readers have repeatedly failed to grasp something so plain?

The mystery of alcoholism in *Tender Is the Night* may be compared to that of the bathroom incident at the Villa Diana. Whatever Violet McKisco witnesses there—something to do with Nicole Diver—is so alarming and so potentially damaging that Tommy Barban fights a duel to protect Nicole's honor. But the secret is withheld until the end of Book One, when the reader becomes a material witness to Nicole's mental breakdown in a Parisian hotel. The purpose of the narrative suspense is to redouble the shock of this second bathroom incident. Along with the naive Rosemary Hoyt, we suddenly understand that chaos yawns beneath the beautifully composed surface of the Divers' world, that their marriage is as fragile as Nicole's sanity.

The secret of Dick's drinking problem is similarly withheld. Although there are a few hints of his vulnerability to alcohol, it does not cause him any obvious trouble until the end of Book Two, when he gets so drunk and disorderly in Rome that Baby Warren must bribe the police to free him from jail. Although Nicole's Parisian crack-up and Dick's Roman binge are structurally parallel scenes—the climaxes, respectively, of Book One and of Book Two—the second lacks the epiphanic power of the first because Fitzgerald does not give Dick's drinking as much thematic importance as Nicole's madness.

—John W. Crowley, *The White Logic: Alcoholism and Gender in American Modernist Fiction* (Amherst: University of Massachusetts Press, 1994): pp. 67–68, 70–73.

Works by
F. Scott Fitzgerald

Fie! Fie! Fi-Fi!, 1914.

The Evil Eye, 1915.

Safety First, 1916.

This Side of Paradise, 1921.

Flappers and Philosophers, 1922.

The Beautiful and Damned, 1922.

Tales of the Jazz Age, 1923.

The Great Gatsby, 1926.

All the Sad Young Men, 1926.

Tender Is the Night, 1934.

Taps at Reveille, 1935.

The Last Tycoon, 1941.

The Crack-Up, 1945.

The Stories of F. Scott Fitzgerald, 1951.

Afternoon of an Author, 1957.

The Pat Hobby Stories, 1962.

Harmondsworth, 1967.

The Letters of F. Scott Fitzgerald, 1963.

The Apprentice Fiction of F. Scott Fitzgerald, 1965.

Thoughtbook of Francis Scott Key Fitzgerald, 1965.

Dearly Beloved, 1970.

F. Scott Fitzgerald in His Own Time: A Miscellany, 1971.

Dear Scott/Dear Max, 1971

As Ever, Scott Fitz, 1972

The Basil and Josephine Stories, 1973.

F. Scott Fitzgerald's Ledger (A Facsimile), 1973

Bits of Paradise, 1973.

Preface to This Side of Paradise, 1973.

The Cruise of the Rolling Junk, 1976.

F. Scott Fitzgerald's Screenplay for Eric Maria Remarque's Three Comrades, 1978.

The Notebooks of F. Scott Fitzgerald, 1978.

F. Scott Fitzgerald's St. Paul Plays, 1978.

The Price Was High, 1979.

Correspondence of F. Scott Fitzgerald, 1980.

Poems 1911–1940, 1981.

The Short Stories of F. Scott Fitzgerald: A New Collection, 1989.

Works about
F. Scott Fitzgerald

Allen, Joan M. *Candles and Carnival Lights: The Catholic Sensibility of F. Scott Fitzgerald.* New York: New York University Press, 1978.

Berman, Ronald. *The Great Gatsby and Modern Times.* Chicago: University of Illinois Press, 1994.

Bigsby, C. W. E. "The Two Identities of F. Scott Fitzgerald." In *The American Novel and the Nineteen Twenties.* London: Edward Arnold, 1971, pp. 129–149.

Bloom, Harold, ed. *F. Scott Fitzgerald's* The Great Gatsby. New York: Chelsea House, 1986.

———, ed. *Modern Critical Views: F. Scott Fitzgerald.* New York: Chelsea House, 1985.

Breitwieser, Mitchell. "*The Great Gatsby:* Grief, Jazz, and the Eye-Witness." *Arizona Quarterly* 47 (Autumn 1991): pp. 17–70.

Bruccoli, Matthew J., ed. *New Essays on The Great Gatsby.* Cambridge: Cambridge University Press, 1985.

———. *Some Sort of Epic Grandeur: The Life of F. Scott Fitzgerald.* New York: Harcourt Brace Jovanovich, 1981.

Bryer, Jackson R., ed. *F. Scott Fitzgerald: The Critical Reception.* New York: Burt Franklin, 1978.

Cartwright, Kent. "Nick Carraway as an Unreliable Narrator." *Papers on Language and Literature: A Journal for Scholars and Critics of Language and Literature* 20, no. 2 (Spring 1984): pp. 218–232.

Claridge, Henry, ed. *F. Scott Fitzgerald: Critical Assessments.* East Sussex: Helm Information, 1991.

Cross, K. G. W. *F. Scott Fitzgerald.* Edinburgh: Oliver and Boyd, 1964; New York: Grove Press, 1964.

Crowley, John W. *The White Logic: Alcoholism and Gender in American Modernist Fiction.* Amherst: University of Massachusetts Press, 1994.

DiBattista, Maria. "The Aesthetic of Forbearance: Fitzgerald's *Tender Is the Night.*" In *American Fiction 1914–1945,* ed. Harold Bloom. New York: Chelsea House, 1986, pp. 209–222.

Eble, Kenneth. *F. Scott Fitzgerald.* In *Twayne's United States Authors Series,* No. 36. Boston: Twayne, 1977.

———. ed. *F. Scott Fitzgerald: A Collection of Criticism.* New York: McGraw-Hill, 1973.

Edwards, Duane. "Who Killed Myrtle Wilson? A Study of *The Great Gatsby.*" *Ball State University Forum* 23, no. 1 (Winter 1982): pp. 35–41.

Ellis, James. "The 'Stoddard Lectures' in *The Great Gatsby.*" *American Literature: A Journal of Literary History, Criticism, and Bibliography* 44 (1972): pp. 470–471.

Fiedler, Leslie. "Some Notes on F. Scott Fitzgerald." In *An End to Innocence.* Boston: Beacon Press, 1955, pp. 174–182.

Fraser, Keath. "Another Reading of *The Great Gatsby.*" In *F. Scott Fitzgerald's The Great Gatsby,* ed. Harold Bloom. New York: Chelsea House, 1986, pp. 57–70.

Fryer, Sarah Beebe. "Fitzgerald's New Women: Harbingers of Change." In *Studies in Modern Literature,* ed. A. Walton Litz and Jackson R. Bryer. Ann Arbor, MI: University of Microfilms, 1988.

Hoffman, Frederick J., ed. *"The Great Gatsby": A Study.* New York: Charles Scribner's, 1962.

Holquist, Michael. "The Inevitability of Stereotype: Colonialism in *The Great Gatsby.*" In *The Rhetoric of Interpretation and the Interpretation of Rhetoric,* ed. Paul Hernadi. Durham, NC: Duke University Press, 1989, pp. 201–220.

Hostetler, Norman H. "From Mayday to Babylon: Disaster, Violence, and Identity in Fitzgerald's Portrait of the 1920s." In *Dancing Fools and Weary Blues: The Great Escape of the Twenties,* ed. R. Lawrence and John D. Walther Broer. Bowling Green, OH: Popular, 1990.

Kazin, Alfred, ed. *F. Scott Fitzgerald: The Man and His Work.* Cleveland: World, 1951.

———. *On Native Grounds.* New York: Reynal and Hitchcock, 1942, pp. 315–323.

Latham, Aaron. *Crazy Sundays: F. Scott Fitzgerald in Hollywood.* New York: Viking Press, 1971.

Lehan, Richard D. *The Great Gatsby: The Limits of Wonder.* In *Twayne's Masterwork Studies,* No. 36. Boston: Twayne, 1990.

———. *F. Scott Fitzgerald and the Craft of Fiction.* Carbondale: Southern Illinois University Press, 1966.

Long, Robert Emmet. *The Achieving of "The Great Gatsby": F. Scott Fitzgerald, 1920–1925.* Lewisburg, PA: Bucknell University Press, 1979.

Michaels, Walter Benn. *Our America: Nativism, Modernism, and Pluralism.* Durham: Duke University Press, 1995.

Miller, James E., Jr. *F. Scott Fitzgerald: His Art and His Technique.* New York: New York University Press, 1964.

Mizener, Arthur. *The Far Side of Paradise: A Biography of F. Scott Fitzgerald.* Revised Edition. Boston: Houghton Mifflin, 1965.

———. ed. *F. Scott Fitzgerald: A Collection of Critical Essays.* Englewood Cliffs, NJ: Prentice-Hall, 1963.

Perosa, Sergio. *The Art of F. Scott Fitzgerald,* trans. Charles Metz and Sergio Perosa. Ann Arbor: University of Michigan Press, 1965.

Petry, Alice Hall. "Fitzgerald's Craft of Short Fiction: The Collected Stories 1920–1935." *Studies in Modern Literature,* No. 103. Ann Arbor: UMI Research Press, 1989.

Piper, Henry Dan. *F. Scott Fitzgerald: A Critical Portrait.* New York: Holt, Rinehart and Winston, 1965.

Rohrkemper, John. "The Allusive Past: Historical Perspective in The Great Gatsby." *College Literature* 12, no. 2 (Spring 1985): pp. 153–162.

Roulston, Robert, and Roulston, Helen H. *The Winding Road to West Egg: the Artistic Development of F. Scott Fitzgerald.* Lewisburg, PA: Bucknell University Press, 1995; London: Associated University Presses, 1995.

Saposnik, Irving S., ed. *The Passion and the Life: Technology as Pattern in The Great Gatsby.* In *Fitzgerald/Hemingway Annual,* ed. Matthew J. Bruccoli and Richard Layman. Detroit: Bruccoli Clark, 1980.

Shain, Charles E. "F. Scott Fitzgerald." In *University of Minnesota Pamphlets on American Writers,* No. 15. Minneapolis: University of Minnesota Press, 1961.

Sklar, Robert. *F. Scott Fitzgerald: The Last Laocoön.* New York: Oxford University Press, 1967.

Stanley, Linda C. *The Foreign Critical Reception of F Scott Fitzgerald: An Analysis and Annotated Bibliography.* Westport, CT: Greenwood Press, 1980.

Untermeyer, Louis. "F. Scott Fitzgerald." In *Makers of the Modern World.* New York: Simon and Schuster, 1955, pp. 691–701.

Way, Brian. *F. Scott Fitzgerald and the Art of Social Fiction.* London: Edward Arnold, 1980.

Wells, Walter. "The Hero and the Hack." In *Tycoons and Locusts: A Regional Look at Hollywood Fiction of the 1930s.* Carbondale: Southern Illinois University Press, 1973, pp. 103–121.

Index of
Themes and Ideas